A Piece of Cake

... und viele weitere Kurzgeschichten
aus dem englischen Alltag

von

Dominic Butler

PONS 10-Minuten-Lektüren ENGLISCH

A Piece of Cake ... und viele weitere
Kurzgeschichten aus dem englischen Alltag

von
Dominic Butler

Alle Personen und Handlungen sind erfunden. Ähnlichkeiten mit lebenden oder verstorbenen Personen und tatsächlichen Begebenheiten wären rein zufällig.

7. Auflage 2025

Projektleitung: Canan Eulenberger-Özdamar
Redaktion: Joanne Popp editing etc., Korntal-Münchingen
Logoentwurf: Erwin Poell, Heidelberg
Logoüberarbeitung: Sabine Redlin, Ludwigsburg
Layout: Petra Michel, Essen
Satz: tebitron gmbh, Gerlingen
Druck: Multiprint Ltd., Kostinbrod

ISBN: 978-3-12-562275-3

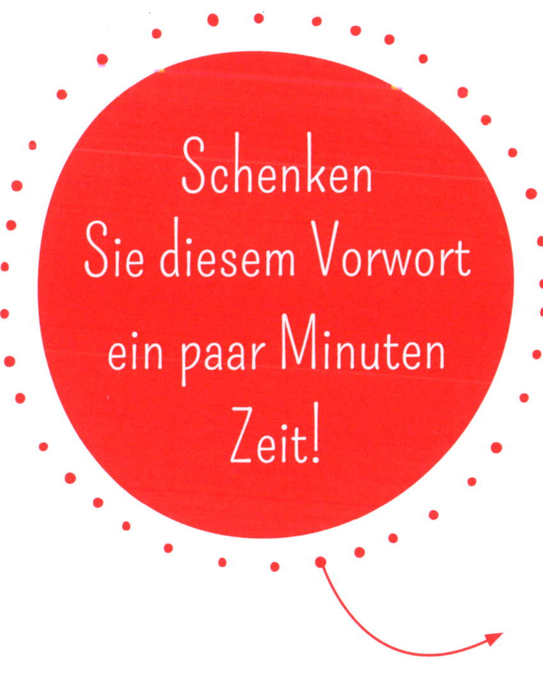
Schenken
Sie diesem Vorwort
ein paar Minuten
Zeit!

Die Geschichten

Perfekt für 10 Minuten!
In diesem Buch finden Sie 15 kurze englische Geschichten, mit denen Sie wunderbar jede Pause, Wartezeit oder Busfahrt verkürzen können.

Mit locker-leichten Geschichten lernen Sie den **englischen Alltag** kennen und erweitern mühelos Ihren Englisch-Wortschatz zu grundlegenden Themen.

Lesefreundlich!
Worthilfen stehen direkt über dem Wort: Haus **house**. So können Sie weiterlesen, ganz ohne Blättern und Suchen im Wörterbuch. Manche Wörter sind **rot** markiert. Das sind Wörter, die in den **Mind-Maps** auftauchen. Dazu mehr auf der nächsten Seite!

Platz für Notizen
Der große Zeilen-abstand bietet auch Raum für Ihre eigenen Eintragungen.

Die Mind-Maps

Das wird Ihr Gehirn lieben!
Unser Gehirn freut sich über Strukturen. Es sortiert Dinge gerne in Gruppen ein, da es sie sich so leichter merken kann.

Natürlicher Gedankengang
Wenn Sie an einen Begriff denken, dann meistens nicht an diesen allein! In der Regel haben Sie, wie auf einer Gedanken-Landkarte (Mind-Map), verwandte Dinge vor Augen.

Wortfelder statt Listen
Auch Wörter lassen sich in thematisch zusammenhängenden Gruppen viel einfacher lernen und merken als in umfangreichen Listen.

Deshalb finden Sie nach jeder Geschichte eine **Mind-Map**, die das zentrale Thema der Geschichte in Form von Vokabeln aufgreift und weiterführt. Hier begegnen Ihnen die rot markierten Wörter aus den Geschichten wieder und viele weitere. Sie sind thematisch gruppiert und liebevoll illustriert.

Viel Spaß & Erfolg beim Entdecken wünscht Ihnen die PONS-Redaktion

INHALT

A Piece of Cake

The restaurant bar was slowly getting busier, while outside the warm summer sun was setting over the River Thames. "This," said Guy, who was holding up his cocktail and looking around the room, "is the perfect hour. It's not too early and not too late. You see, any earlier than this, and people aren't relaxed enough. You need to wait until they've had a drink or two and he started to **sway** (hin und her wiegen) to the music. Of course, if you are too late, then people are too relaxed. Too many drinks are never a good thing. Too late in the evening, all people want to do is dance with their friends and drink even more. You see, **flirting** (flirten) with someone is like a dance; it's all about timing." He smiled then, **obviously** (offenbar) enjoying his own advice.

He was not a very tall man, but maybe just a little taller than average. His hair was straight and **gelled** (gegelt), with just the

(hier:) leichte Spur Schläfen
slightest hint of grey at his dark **temples**. His skin was lightly gebräunt **tanned**, his teeth a little whiter than normal. He was also very fit, and his blue summer shirt seemed to be a size too small for him. "You can write that down, you know. You need all the help you can get," he laughed loudly, and the man next to him smiled a little. Ich mache nur Spaß "**Only kidding**, Toby. (hier:) Halte dich an mich **You stick with me**; you'll be a (hier:) Aufreißer, Frauenheld **player** one day."

Toby was a shorter, slightly younger man, with brown hair, an honest, simple face and kind eyes. "Oh, I don't really want to be a player, Guy. It'd just be nice to meet someone."

"Sure, sure. No problem at all. All you have to do is watch and learn, my friend."

Toby wasn't entirely sure if he was Guy's friend. They had played golf together a few times. Guy had geschummelt **cheated** twice but Toby hadn't said anything. He'd also made some rather sexist jokes that Toby didn't like. In fact, after the second game, Toby had decided to (hier:) aus dem Weg gehen **avoid** Guy when possible, but somehow Guy had got his phone number, called him, and told him they were going out to find some women. Toby had tried to say no, but after ten minutes he'd **given up** (aufgegeben) and agreed to meet in this **swanky** (schick) central London bar.

"Now, what's your best **chat-up line** (Anmachspruch)?" asked Guy.

"My what?"

"Your chat-up line? You know, what do you say to **seduce** (verführen) the ladies?"

"I don't know. **I introduce myself** (Ich stelle mich vor.). Sometimes **I pay them a compliment** (ich mache ihnen ein Kompliment)."

Guy laughed loudly and **slapped** (klopfte) Toby on the back with such force that he nearly dropped his beer. "Oh my God! You "introduce" yourself? Toby, Toby, Toby; this isn't some business conference in Brighton. You're not networking for new clients. This is the game of love. It's a dangerous, **competitive** (konkurrierend) world. No, you need something special. You need something that's going to **catch their attention** (ihre Aufmerksamkeit erregen)."

Toby took a long drink of beer. Maybe he could say he was going to the bathroom and **sneak out** (hinausschleichen). He could catch the bus home in time to watch that documentary that was on Channel 4.

"Well, aren't you going to ask me what I do?" said Guy.

Du verabredest dich mit ihnen?
"**You ask them out on a date?**" said Toby.

Guy laughed again. "It's not that simple, Toby. A woman wants to be **impressed** (beeindruckt). They want to be **chased** ((hier:) umworben). Of course, I've got a few different **moves** ((hier:) Schachzüge), for a few different situations, but ..."

Guy looked around the room then. "But I do have one move that never fails."

"Really?" said Toby, who was thinking about what take-away he should get.

"Yes, remember? I was telling you about it when we were playing golf." Guy **clicked his fingers** (schnipste mit den Fingern) at a waiter who was walking past.

The waiter's face became **instantly** (sofort) unhappy, but the poor man stopped. "Yes, sir. Can I get you something?"

"Yes. Get me a piece of cake. Something **creamy** (sahnig). If you can throw a cherry on top, even better. Quickly now."

The waiter moved away; his face even unhappier. Toby was about to tell Guy that he shouldn't speak to people like that, but Guy raised a finger and **shushed** (sagte, dass er still sein soll) him before he could speak.

"There, do you see her?" he asked. "Straight ahead. What a fine

Exemplar
specimen." Guy was looking at an attractive, dark-haired woman who was standing near the bar with a group of friends. "Right, here I go. Watch and learn, Toby." And without another word Guy was walking across the bar. When he saw the waiter returning with the piece of cake on a nice plate, he took it and sent the poor man away without a single thank you.

"Is your friend always like that?" Toby heard someone say.

He turned around and saw a pretty young lady watching Guy stolzieren **strut** across the room. "Oh, he's not my friend. In fact, I think he's the worst person I've ever met ... but yes, he's always like that."

"What's he going to do with the cake?"

Toby thought for a moment. "I don't exactly remember. He did tell me about it. I think he tells the woman that she is just like a piece of cake; great to look at, lecker **delicious** and befriedigend **satisfying**."

"And the cherry?" asked the young woman, who Toby thought seemed very nice indeed.

"Oh, he says that the cherry on top is that he would like to buy her a drink, so lucky her."

The woman laughed. "And does it work?"

Toby laughed. "I hope not. Maybe we should go and watch?"

And when the young woman smiled, they quickly walked across the bar together and reached Guy and the dark-haired lady just in time to hear her say something.

"I'm just like a piece of cake? What ... easy?" she said, and before Guy could reply, the woman took the plate off him and pushed the creamy cake into his face.

brachen in Lachen aus

Toby and his new friend **burst into laughter** and quickly moved away. "My name's Toby, by the way," he said.

"Sally."

"What a lovely name. I don't suppose you like documentaries, do you?"

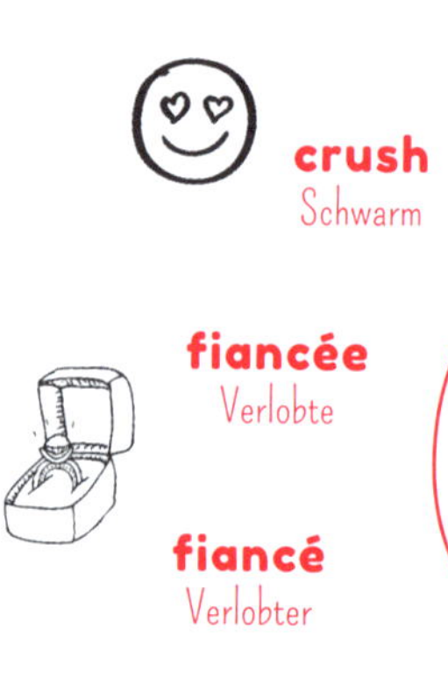

describing a partner

eine/n Partner/in beschreiben

crush
Schwarm

date
Date, Verabredung

girlfriend
Freundin

fiancée
Verlobte

fiancé
Verlobter

boyfriend
Freund

wife
Ehefrau

husband
Ehemann

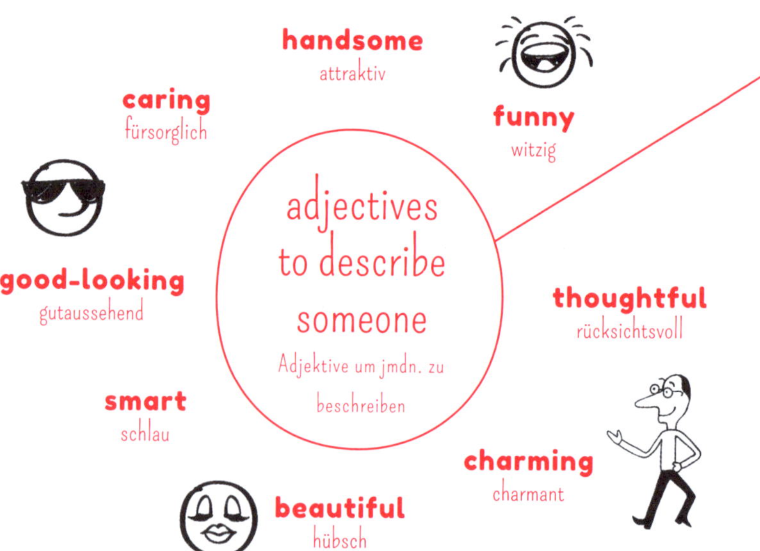

adjectives to describe someone

Adjektive um jmdn. zu beschreiben

handsome
attraktiv

caring
fürsorglich

funny
witzig

good-looking
gutaussehend

thoughtful
rücksichtsvoll

smart
schlau

charming
charmant

beautiful
hübsch

to pay sb. a compliment
jmdm. ein Kompliment machen

to cheat on sb.
jmdn. betrügen

common expressions
häufige Ausdrücke

to date sb.
mit jmdm. ausgehen

to be a player
ein/e Aufreißer/in sein

to break up with sb.
sich von jmdm. trennen

to fall for sb.
sich in jmdn. verknallen

to flirt with sb.
mit jmdm. flirten

to chat sb. up
jmdn. anmachen

to ask sb. out (on a date)
sich mit jmdm. verabreden

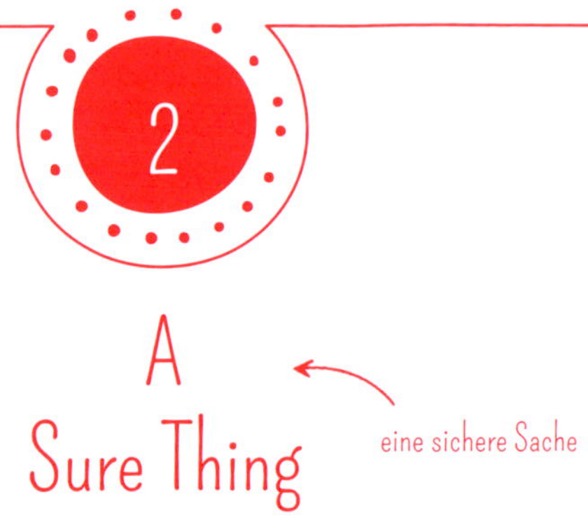

2 A Sure Thing

eine sichere Sache

The rain was starting to slow now, and on the course, the jockeys were moving their horses into position. It would be a few minutes before the next race **though** (jedoch), so Terry turned back to his newspaper and looked at the **crossword** (Kreuzworträtsel).

"Here you are," said Gerry. "That'll warm you up."

Terry looked up at Gerry, who was walking back to their seats with two cups of hot tea. Terry and Gerry were not brothers but could easily **pretend** (vorgeben) they were if they wanted to. They were both middle-aged men with grey hair, dark eyes and **thick** ((hier:) stark) Irish accents. "Cheers, Gerry. Looks like we'll have a race in a minute or two."

Gerry nodded and sat down. The viewing area was quiet today, with just a few of the regulars sitting and watching the **course** ((hier:) Rennbahn) without much interest. "Hey, what have we got here?" asked

Gerry, who **spotted** (erspähte) a stranger walking in their direction.

The stranger was a tall man dressed in formal clothes. He had a pair of large **binoculars** (Fernglas (im Englischen immer Pl.)) round his neck, a **smart** ((hier:) schick) **flat cap** (Schiebermütze), and a slightly confused expression on his face.

"I **bet** (wette) he's English," Gerry said.

Terry nodded. "I won't bet on that; it's a sure thing."

The two men laughed quietly, then turned their eyes down when the man got closer, hoping they wouldn't be seen.

"Excuse me," said the stranger, in a polite English accent. "**I don't suppose** (Ich frage mich, ob) you could help me, could you?"

Gerry and Terry **sighed** (seufzten). "What's the problem?"

The man's rather simple face **lit up** (hellte sich auf). "Well, it's my first time here, **you see** (wissen Sie). First time at any races, actually. I'd like to **put a bet on** (eine Wette auf ein Rennen setzen), but I don't know what to do. Can I bet on this race?" he said, pointing down at the field where the horses were lining up.

Terry shook his head. "**Probably not** (Wahrscheinlich nicht.). It's a about to start. I don't think you'll get to the kiosk in time."

The English man looked disappointed. "That's a shame. I have all this money, you see," he said, showing them a thick roll of euros. Terry and Gerry wechselten einen kurzen Blick **exchanged a quick look**. There were two things that they loved most in this life, betting on the horses and winning money from the English.

"Well," said Terry. "We were thinking of having a little bet on this race, too. Why don't the three of us make a bet?"

The English man's smile almost made Gerry laugh. "Really? That'd be toll **smashing**. Now, who do you think will win? Meinst du/Meinen Sie **Do you reckon** it could be that grey down there? He looks like seine Chancen stehen gut **he's got a good chance**."

Terry and Gerry coughed. They actually thought that the grey had a very good chance, so they didn't want their new friend to bet on that. "Ah, well now, he's a pretty little horse, but I don't know if you want to bet on him. I don't think he's going to do well on this wet grass," lied Terry.

"Ah, right. Well, what about number 10? Denkst du/Denken Sie, dass es wahrscheinlich ist, dass er ins Ziel kommt? **Do you think he's likely to finish**?"

"Oh yes," said Gerry. "He'll finish, but he might take his time. He's quite old, you see." This was not true. Number 10 was

Gerry's favourite to win.

"Damn. Well, that's no good, is it? I want one of those ... what do you call it ... a sure thing?"

Gerry and Terry nearly laughed again. "Yes, that'd be nice, wouldn't it? Well. That brown one down there, number 13, he's pretty close to being a sure thing."

The English man raised his binoculars to his face. "What? The one at the end? But ... but he's not even facing the right way. His jockey can't make him look forwards."

"Er ... well, you see ..." said Gerry, who lowered his voice. "That's just an old racing trick. They do that so the **odds** (Gewinnchancen) on him go down, then someone puts a big bet on at the last minute. It's a sure sign that he's got a good chance."

There was a bit of action down on the course, which Terry pointed to. "Look, it's about to start. If we're going to bet, now's the time. How much did we say? 100 for a win? 50 for second or third?"

"So little?" asked Gerry. "But the man wants a real bet, right? What about 200 for the win, 100 for second and third?"

The English man **hesitated** (zögerte) for a second. "Hurry up, now. It's about to start."

"Well, OK then. And I guess I'll take number 13. What's its name?"

"Er ... **No Chance in Hell** (Nicht die geringste Chance) ... I believe," Gerry said, hiding his smile behind his newspaper. "But **what's in a name** (Namen sind Schall und Rauch), right?"

The English man looked a little less sure now. "Oh, right. And you **chaps** (Burschen)? Who are you betting on?"

"Well, **since** (da) it's your first time, and you don't really know what you're doing, why don't I take number 10 and Terry take the little grey? OK? Great. It's a bet!"

And before the English man knew what was happening, they were shaking hands and a **gunshot** (Schuss) **signalled** (signalisierte) the start of the race.

After that, everything seemed to happen so quickly that later the English man would find it hard to describe it to his friends. He remembered standing up and **cheering** (jubeln), watching the twenty horses racing around the wet grass of the Dublin racccourse and the thin Irish rain still falling. He remembered that no one else was cheering, but he didn't really care. If he was honest, he didn't even know where his horse was for most of the race. He forgot to use his binoculars and just enjoyed the whole thing. But then, when the first horse crossed the line, he heard some familiar words **announced** (bekanntgegeben) on the **Tannoy® system** (Lautsprecheranlage):

"I can't believe it ... No Chance in Hell wins his first ever race! No one could have **predicted** (vorhergesagt) it, but he's won! He's won!"

And he remembers the confused faces of the two nice Irish men, and the way they didn't really say a word as they handed him his 400 euros.

Yes, it really was one of the best mornings of his life; that was a sure thing.

might
könnte
modal verbs
Modalverben
may
könnte
could
könnte
predictions
Vorhersagen
Do you think ...?
Meinst du/Meinen Sie ...?
useful phrases
nützliche Sätze
It's very unlikely.
Es ist sehr unwahrscheinlich.
Do you reckon ...?
Meinst du/Meinen Sie ...?
My guess is ...
Ich denke ...

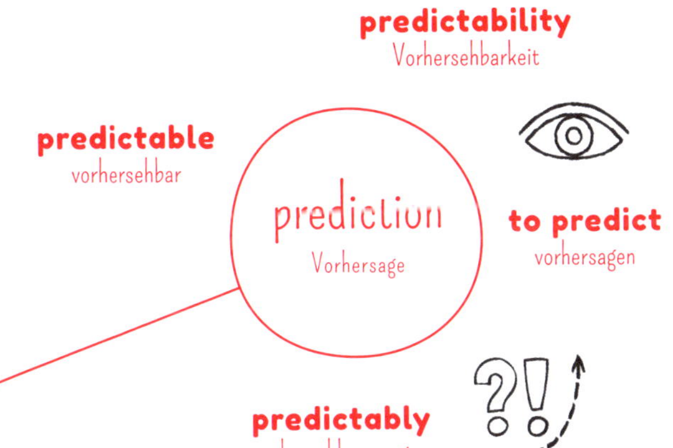
predictability
Vorhersehbarkeit
predictable
vorhersehbar
prediction
Vorhersage
to predict
vorhersagen
predictably
vorhersehbarerweise

a sure thing
eine sichere Sache
likely to
wahrscheinlich, dass
probability
Wahrscheinlichkeit
will probably
wird wahrscheinlich
to bet on
wetten
a good chance
eine gute Chance
probably not
wahrscheinlich nicht
idea

The Culture Shock

Kulturschock

It was the jet lag; that was the problem.

Normally, Chrissie was a good traveller. She wasn't one of those English people who only spoke English when abroad. No, she always learnt a few **phrases** (Wendungen), how to say please and thank you, how to ask for something in a shop. Also, she always tried to learn a little bit about the country before she went there, their **habits and customs** (Gewohnheiten und Bräuche), whether they **shook hands** (die Hand gaben) or **kissed cheeks** (beide Wangen küssten) or **bowed** (sich verbeugten). It was, Chrissie thought, the right thing to do. It just made things a lot **smoother** (einfacher). And Chrissie liked things to be smooth. She liked them to be smooth, simple and organised.

On this trip, however, it seemed like nothing was smooth, simple or organised. From the moment she landed in Japan, things had been going wrong. They lost her luggage at the airport. The taxi couldn't find her hotel. And, after waking up half an hour late, she nearly didn't get to the meeting with her important **Japanese** (japanische) **clients** (Kunden) on time. Yes, she had just about made it, but when she **rushed** (eilte) into the room, everyone, including her boss, looked at her like she was a late, unorganised mess.

"You have to understand," her boss had said later. "In their **culture** (Kultur), **punctuality** (Pünktlichkeit) is very important."

"I know that, Jill," Chrissie had said. "It won't happen again."

Jill had nodded but looked at her worriedly. "We need these clients, Chrissie. We really need them. Without them ..."

Jill hadn't said anything else. She didn't have to. Chrissie was **determined** (entschlossen) that nothing else would go wrong.

The next morning, when she awoke, however, she still couldn't **shake the horrible feeling** (das schreckliche Gefühl abschütteln) that everything was going to be a **disaster** (Katastrophe) again.

"It's just the jetlag," she repeated in the taxi. But when she looked at her watch, and then at the slow traffic that they were in, she **realised** (realisierte) there was a chance she might be late again.

"I'm so sorry," she said to the taxi driver, "Can you go faster?

I need to get to the restaurant by 1 o'clock."

The driver didn't seem to understand, and Chrissie hated that she hadn't learnt some more of the language. Sitting back, she took her notepad from her bag and looked at some of the Japanese customs that she had made a note of. She had eingekreist **circled** a note about bowing when she met someone, another note about Visitenkarten austauschen **exchanging business cards** and another about Augenkontakt herstellen **making eye-contakt**. She was trying to remember this important information when the taxi turned left and she saw her destination. She was about to put her notes on kulturell **cultural** Unterschiede **differences** away when something caught her eye. There was a note about karaoke. She didn't remember the tip, but it said that at business lunches, it was common that people would get up and sing a few songs to das Eis brechen **break the ice** or to celebrate making a deal.

Chrissie felt suddenly very worried. She hated singing. She was pretty sure that she had the worst voice in the world. But surely, she thought to herself, they wouldn't be going to a karaoke bar for lunch, would they?

Just as the taxi was **pulling up** (anhielt), Jill sent her a message.

"Where are you? We're about to start."

Chrissie gave some money to the taxi driver and told him to **keep the change** (das Rückgeld behalten). However, he seemed very unhappy about this idea and took his time slowly counting out her change. Brilliant, she thought, another custom that she had **messed up** (vermasselt).

As soon as he had given her the last coin, she jumped out of the taxi and ran to the restaurant. She was almost at the door when she looked up and saw the sign at the top of the building, it read: "Kagura Karaoke Restaurant".

"No, no, no!" she said. "Not this! I'd do anything for the company ... but not this."

Then she remembered Jill's face the day before, and how worried she'd looked about getting these new clients.

"Fine," she said, and although she felt more scared than she had for years, she knew what she had to do.

She pushed open the door of the restaurant, bowed to the manager and asked to be shown to the table. As she was being led down a corridor with several doors on both sides, she could hear someone singing and her stomach **tightened** (zog sich zusammen). Just as the manager stopped to open one of the doors, the singing stopped and she heard people **clapping** (klatschen).

The manager opened the door and Chrissie stepped inside. Her other colleagues, and the Japanese clients, were all sitting around a table on the floor, their shoes off. Jill was standing at the front of the room, a microphone in her hand. "Ah, Chrissie, there you are. You're just in time. It's your turn to ..."

But Chrissie didn't need to let her finish. She knew what she had to do. She took hold of the microphone, pulled off her shoes and looked around at the audience. For a moment, when no music began, she **hesitated** (zögerte). But when she looked at Jill and saw her boss nodding her head, she knew it was now or never ... and she started to sing.

It was her favourite song. She hadn't sung it for years, but suddenly she was there, singing it at the top of her voice, without music, missing every note, getting most of the words wrong and looking **ridiculous** (lächerlich).

But ... she realised ... she was actually enjoying it.

And it was only when she had finished all three Strophen **verses** and two Refrains **choruses** of the song, that she realised that everyone was looking at her with expressions of absolute shock on their faces.

There was a second of silence, then Jill moved over to her and flüsterte **whispered** in her ear, "I was saying ... it's your turn ... to introduce yourself."

From the room across the corridor, she heard someone starting to sing and she realised her mistake.

Then, Mr Tanaka, the boss of the clients they were trying to beeindrucken **impress**, slowly stood up, his face serious.

"I'm so s..." Chrissie began to say.

But she never got to finish her apology, because Mr Tanaka began to clap and a large smile breitete sich aus **spread across** his face.

And then his colleagues were standing and clapping too.

And Chrissie didn't remember much after that. Except that she sang another three songs, drank quite a lot of sake and watched Jill and Mr Tanaka sign the company's biggest ever deal.

ethnicity
Ethnizität

culture
Kultur

traditions
Traditionen

useful vocabulary

nützliche Wörter

stereotypes
Stereotype

habits
Gewohnheiten

rites
Riten

to bow
sich verbeugen

to tip sb.
jmdm. Trinkgeld geben

to kiss cheeks
beide Wangen küssen

customs

Bräuche

to make eye contact
Augenkontakt herstellen

to shake hands
die Hand geben

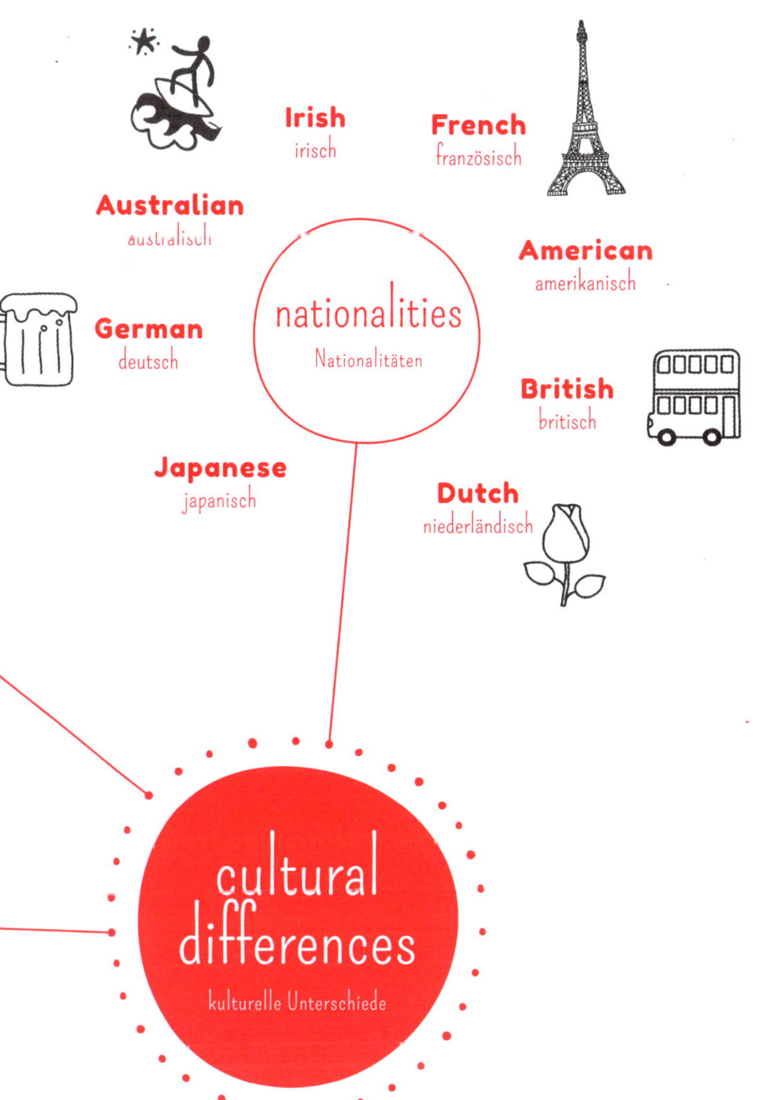
Irish
irisch
French
französisch
Australian
australisch
American
amerikanisch
German
deutsch
nationalities
Nationalitäten
British
britisch
Japanese
japanisch
Dutch
niederländisch
cultural differences
kulturelle Unterschiede

Meet Me in the Middle

As soon as David pushed the window open, he knew that this was going to be a hard day. He looked out across the city of Liverpool at the grey Mersey river and he **wondered** (fragte sich), not for the first time, if he should find another job.

"Well?" the Chief Inspector said. "Are you going or not?"

"Yes ... **I suppose so** (ich denke schon)," he said, unhappily.

"We've got you on this," said an officer, who was attaching a **safety harness** (Sicherheitsgurt) to his **waist** (Taille). "But try not to fall. There's a good chance you'll hit the wall and break an arm if you do."

"Brilliant," David **muttered** (murmelte), then he stepped out onto the **ledge** (Sims) of the Liver Building and tried not to look down.

Slowly he began to move to his left, his back against the wall, his feet dangerously close to the **edge** (Kante).

"How high is this exactly?" he called back to the faces at the window.

"About 40 metres," an officer shouted back.

David shook his head unhappily and continued to slowly move along the building. After a few more minutes, he got to a corner and as he was moving around it, he heard someone shout, "Stay back!"

David nodded, but moved a little more so that he could see the person. "I won't come any closer," he said to the man who was sitting on the ledge. He was a young man, probably no more than 26 or 27 years old, with **scruffy** (ungepflegt) black hair, sad brown eyes and a cheap suit. In his hands, he was holding a picture of a young woman, and when David saw it, he thought he knew what this was all about. "She's pretty," he said. "Girlfriend?"

"Fiancée. **At least** (Zumindest), she was. She was **supposed to** (sollte) meet me here today. We were going to get married ... but ..."

"She didn't **turn up** (auftauchen). Did you try calling her?"

The man looked at him like he was stupid. "Only like a hundred times. She won't **pick up** (abheben). She's changed her mind. She doesn't love me anymore. And if she doesn't love me anymore, then ..."

And David saw the young man look down. "Wait! Wait a second. Just one second, yeah? I mean, if you jump now, before I get to do my job, it makes me look really bad."

The young man looked up at him. "Why? What's your job?"

David blinked. "I'm a window cleaner."

"Really?"

"No! Not really. I'm a **negotiator** (Vermittler).

"A negotiator? I've never heard of that. What exactly do you do?"

David **shrugged** (zuckte mit den Achseln). "Well, this, normally. Sometimes I speak to criminals, you know, people robbing banks. They normally have **hostages** (Geiseln) and want something, like a plane or a promise they won't go to jail. I try to get them to **compromise** (einen Kompromiss schließen), then meet me in the middle."

"Meet you in the middle?"

"Yeah, I **negotiate** (verhandle). I try to keep them calm. That sort of thing."

"Right," said the young man, who didn't really seem to understand. "So why are you here talking to me? I mean, how can I meet you in the middle? I'm going to jump off this building. Are you going to ask me to jump halfway or something?"

David **got the impression** (bekam den Eindruck) that the young man was not the cleverest person in the world. "Well, no ..."

"And do you like your job? It seems a bit dangerous to me. And, well, maybe a bit **pointless** (sinnlos). I mean, if someone wants to jump, you should just let them jump. It's their life, isn't it? I don't think I'd do your job."

David wasn't sure why the conversation was going this way, but the first rule in this type of situation was to keep the person talking, so that's what he was going to do. "Well, I help people ... sometimes. So that's nice."

"Oh," said the young man. "But I **suppose** (denke) you get a lot of money."

David shrugged and told him how much he earned, which he **regretted** (bereute), as the young man began to laugh. "That's not very much is it? You want to ask for a pay rise. I'm sure you can **persuade** (überreden) them to give you a bit more.

There was a strong breeze and David felt it push him. "You know what, maybe you're right," he said, suddenly feeling very unhappy about things. "I mean, what am I doing with my life? Am I ever going to get a promotion? Am I going to be climbing out onto ledges like this forever? You know, I tried to **convince** (überzeugen) my boss to give me a **promotion** (Beförderung) a few weeks ago, but he wouldn't even listen to my proposal. You know ..."

David was about to say something, when from the street below, there was a **terrible scream** (schrecklicher Schrei), "Gary!"

The young man on the ledge looked down. A crowd of people were watching the situation and a pretty young lady was pushing through them.

"Stacey?" the man on the ledge said. "Stacey!"

"Gary," the woman shouted up. "What are you doing?"

"I'm going to ... well ... you know. I mean, without you, **there's no point in living** (es gibt keinen Grund zum Weiterleben)!"

"Without me? What are you talking about? I'm here. I thought we were getting married!"

"Yeah, at 11.00 o'clock. I waited an hour for you and you never turned up. I called you a hundred times and you didn't answer."

"11? Gary, we're getting married at 1! I wrote it all down for you. And yeah, I didn't answer my phone because last night me and the girls went out for some drinks and I lost it."

The expression on the young man's face **changed dramatically** (änderte sich dramatisch). "You mean ... you still love me? You still want to get married?"

"Of course, I do!" Stacey shouted, and the people in the crowd began to **cheer** (jubeln).

In a second, Gary was standing and slowly moving along the ledge. David, who had watched the whole thing in **disbelief** (fassungslos), was shaking his head. "This job really is **ridiculous** (lächerlich)," he said.

"Hey, look," said Gary, as he was getting closer. "I'm meeting you in the middle."

David did not laugh at his joke.

"Well, should we go back in?" Gary asked, when he reached him.

David thought for a second. "You go in," he said, then sat down on the ledge and looked out across the city, unhappily. "I think I might just stay here and think for a while."

Gary shrugged and kept on moving. He thought that the negotiator seemed like a rather odd sort of man. But then, there were a lot of odd people out there these days.

useful expressions
nützliche Ausdrücke

IDEA !?

to accept/reject a proposal
einen Vorschlag annehmen/ablehnen

to make a concession
ein Zugestandnis machen

to compromise
einen Kompromiss schließen

to meet in the middle
sich in der Mitte treffen

to reach an agreement
sich einigen

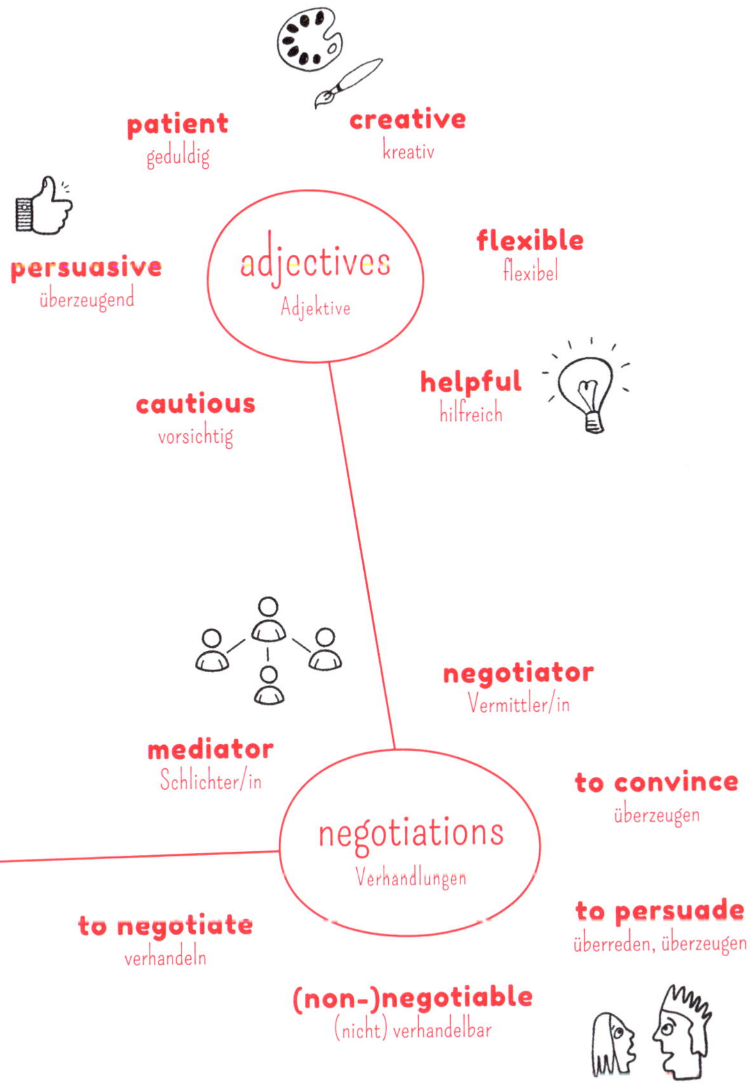

patient
geduldig
creative
kreativ
persuasive
überzeugend
adjectives
Adjektive
flexible
flexibel
helpful
hilfreich
cautious
vorsichtig
negotiator
Vermittler/in
mediator
Schlichter/in
to convince
überzeugen
negotiations
Verhandlungen
to persuade
überreden, überzeugen
to negotiate
verhandeln
(non-)negotiable
(nicht) verhandelbar

The Fairy Tale

Märchen

The rain was still falling, and the two children sitting on the sofa by the window seemed very unhappy about it.

On the other side of the room, in her favourite chair next to the fire, their grandmother, Elizabeth Axton, looked at them and put down her **knitting** (Strickzeug). "Why don't you two play a board game? There are lots in the cupboard."

Peter, the older child, looked at his younger brother Michael, and they both shook their heads. "We don't really like board games anymore, Grandma. We like computer games now."

Elizabeth smiled. "I see. Well, I don't have one of those computer things here, so you'll have to find something else to do." The boys **nodded** (nickte), rather unhappily. "You could read a book. You used to love some of the old story books that I have upstairs."

Peter **shrugged** (zuckte mit den Achseln). "They're OK, but they're not as good as movies, are they? We watch a lot of movies now."

"Ah," said Elizabeth. "Well, I don't have a television, do I?"

"We know that," said Michael, with a **bored expression** (gelangweilter Ausdruck) on his young face. "It's OK."

The two boys turned back to the window and Elizabeth **sighed** (seufzte). When they came to visit on sunny days, they always enjoyed themselves, but on days like this they were getting **harder and** (immer schwerer) **harder to please** (zufriedenzustellen).

She picked up her **knitting needles** (Stricknadeln) and was about to start working on the jumper again, when she saw the old **scar** (Narbe) on the top of her hand. She looked at it for a moment, and a strange expression came across her face. "Boys," she said, quite quietly. "Have I ever told you how I got this scar on my hand?"

The boys shook their heads again, but continued to **stare** (starren) at the rain, uninterested. "Well, I'll tell you all about it, if you like. It's only a short story, and not a very interesting **tale** (Geschichte), I'm sure, but maybe it'll pass a little time."

"OK, Grandma," said Peter, in a bored voice.

Elizabeth smiled. "Well, let me **set the scene** (den Rahmen abstecken). See, it happened a very long time ago, on a day very much like this. I was about your age Michael, and one wet Sunday afternoon I was sitting in this room looking out of the window, just like you two are now."

"You lived here when you were a child?" asked Peter.

"I've lived in this house my gesamtes Leben **entire life**, Peter. Didn't you know that?"

The boy shrugged and Elizabeth continued. "Well, it had been raining all morning, but an hour after lunch the clouds verschwanden **disappeared** and the sun came out. I was looking at a rainbow at the far end of the garden when I saw something strange down by that apple tree. Do you see it?"

The boys got up on their knees on the sofa and looked out of the window into the rain. "I see it," said Michael, sounding a little more interested now. "What did you see?"

"Well, just for a second, I thought I saw a very small person down there. I thought that perhaps one of the children from the village was trying to steal our apples. I shouted for my mother, but when she didn't reply, I pulled on my Gummistiefel **wellington boots** and raincoat, and I went outside."

"What happened next?" asked Michael.

"I'll tell you, but you won't believe me. You see, I started to walk down the path. I was walking quite slowly, because the stones were wet and I was a little bit scared. I don't know why, but something in the air felt strange. It didn't feel like my garden. Do you know what I mean?"

Neither boy replied, but they both looked interested now, though Peter had an **expression of disbelief** (Ausdruck der Ungläubigkeit) on his face.

"So, I walked closer to the apple tree and do you know what I saw? I saw a pair of hands reaching out around the tree. As soon as I saw them, I stopped. *Who's there?* I called out. But there was no reply. I took one step closer and then I could see the hands much clearer. The fingers were tiny, with sharp little **claws** (Krallen) where the **fingernails** (Fingernägel) should be. And the arms were very thin, with a golden bracelet on one wrist. As soon as I saw that golden bracelet, I knew who ... or what ... was behind that tree."

She stopped speaking then, and for a moment there was only the sound of the rain against the window and the **crackling** (Knistern) of the fire. "Who ... what was it, Grandma?" asked Michael.

"Well, I'd heard many **myths and yarns** (Märchen und Geschichten) about them, you see. My grandmother had warned me that on rainy days, when the sun comes out and the rainbows fill the sky, they come out of their world and into ours. And you know, they're not like they are in those story books upstairs. No, in reality they are horrible dangerous little **creatures** (Kreaturen). **At best** (Im besten Fall), they **play cruel jokes** (treiben grausame Scherze) on you, or steal any gold that might be in the house. But **at worst** (im schlimmsten Fall), well, at worst they take babies and small children back to their own world to be their **slaves** (Sklaven) for all **eternity** (Ewigkeit)."

The children were on the **edge of their seat** (Sitzkante) now, listening to her every word and **hooked on her narrative** (hingen an jedem Wort ihrer Geschichte). "What? What was it? What was behind the tree?"

She **leaned forwards** (beugte sich nach vorne); her face serious. "A fairy."

Peter laughed then, but the sound was a **little forced** (etwas gezwungen). "But fairies aren't real, Grandma. They're **made up** (erfunden). They're just **fiction** ((hier:) Erfindung)."

Elizabeth shrugged. "Maybe you're right. Maybe they don't exist now. I haven't seen one for a very long time. But I saw one that day; that's the truth."

"What did you do, Grandma?" asked Michael.

"I was very silly, Michael. I wanted to see all of it, so I reached out and took hold of its arm. There was a terrible scream as soon as I touched it, then the next thing I know, it pulled its hand away and schlug **struck** me with its claws. I screamed then too, and after a second my mother ran out to the garden and took me back inside."

Michael's eyes were vor Aufregung weit aufgerissen **wide with excitement**, and even Peter seemed happy with her little Anekdote **anecdote**.

"Oh, look, the sun's coming out. I wonder if there might be a rainbow," she said.

"We might see a fairy!" shouted Michael. "Can we go outside, Grandma?"

"Sure. But stay together. And if you do see one, don't get too close."

Michael ran out of the room to put his boots on, but Peter stopped for a moment, a smile on his face. "Was it a real story, Grandma?"

Elizabeth picked up her knitting needles again and looked at the scar on her hand. "Maybe," she said. "Or maybe it was just a fairy tale."

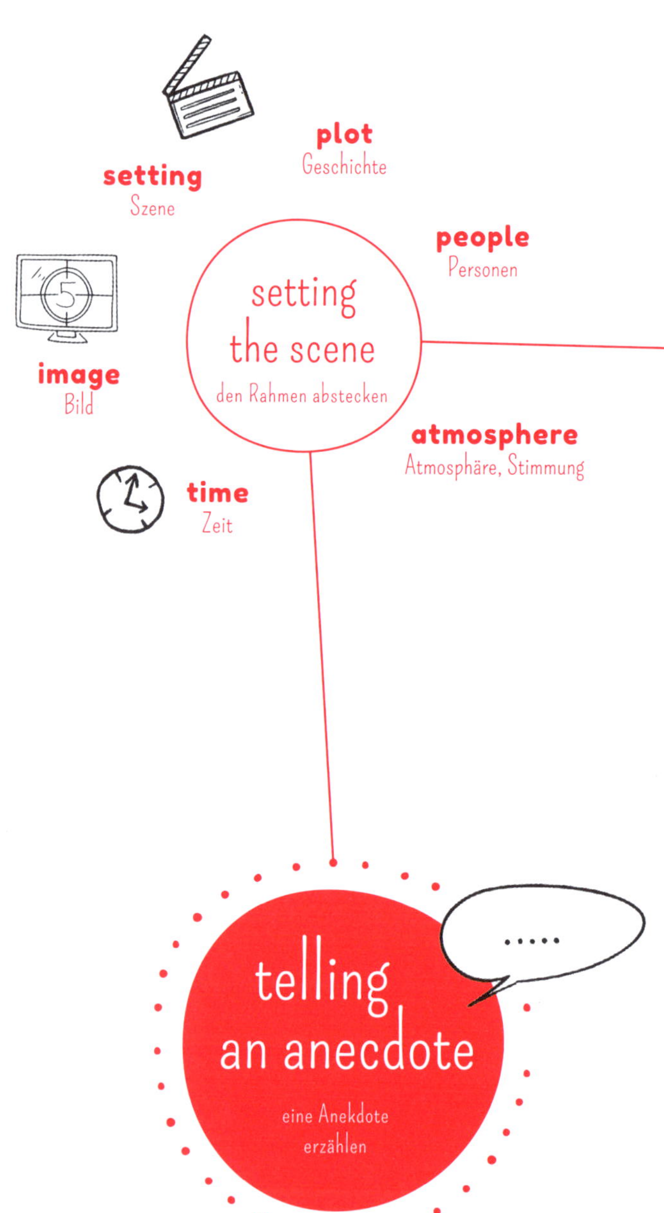
plot
Geschichte
setting
Szene
people
Personen
setting the scene
den Rahmen abstecken
image
Bild
atmosphere
Atmosphäre, Stimmung
time
Zeit
telling an anecdote
eine Anekdote erzählen
.....

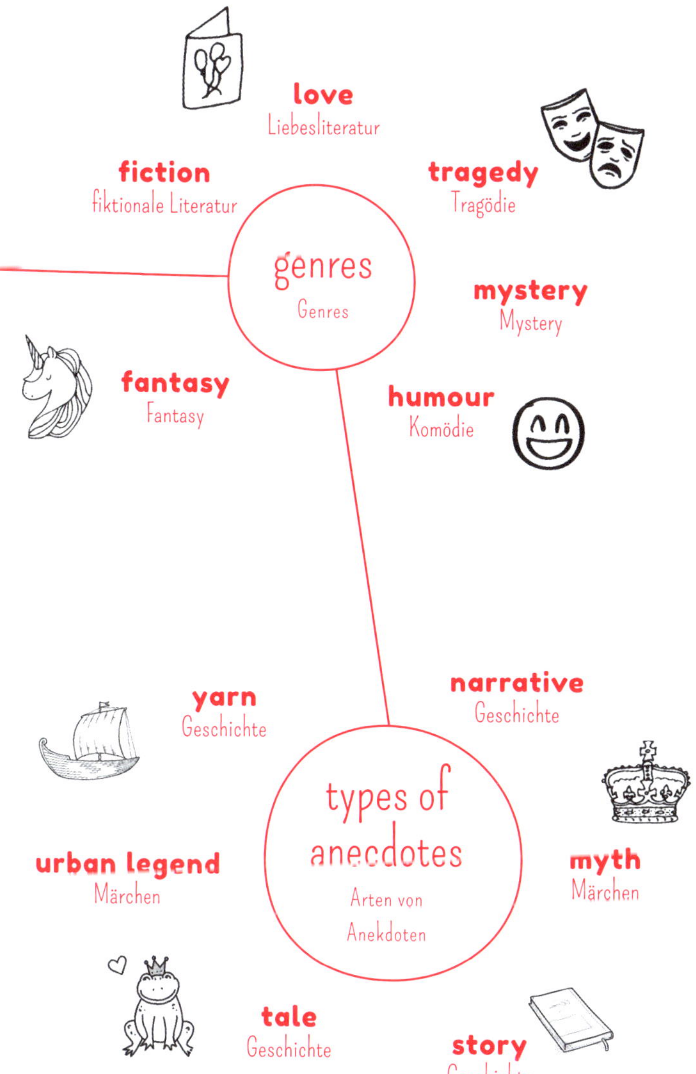
love
Liebesliteratur
fiction
fiktionale Literatur
tragedy
Tragödie
genres
Genres
mystery
Mystery
fantasy
Fantasy
humour
Komödie
yarn
Geschichte
narrative
Geschichte
types of anecdotes
Arten von Anekdoten
urban legend
Märchen
myth
Märchen
tale
Geschichte
story
Geschichte

The Team Leader

When the schrecklich **terrifying** video stopped playing, there was silence in the small office.

Then, "What are we going to do, Henry?" asked Mary Watts, his HR manager.

"Yeah," said his secretary Martin. "The video said we need to get out of here, but, how can we?"

The six or seven other employees from Hale Ltd all turned to look at Geschäftsführer (‚CEO' ist die Abkürzung für ‚chief executive officer') **CEO** Henry Hale, and he knew what they wanted. They wanted him to be their leader.

He was about to open his mouth to speak, when all of his Bedenken und Ängste **doubts and fears** came back to him. It was Henry's biggest problem. He was a great CEO in many ways; he was organisiert **organised**, creative and he verstand sich gut **got on well with** all of his employees. The only problem was, he didn't have very good

leadership skills (Führungsqualifikationen). He was quite an **indecisive** (unentschlossen) person. When he did have to make a decision, he did it very slowly and would often **change his mind** (seine Meinung ändern) a few times.

"**It's up to you** (Es ist dir/Ihnen überlassen), Henry," Mary said.

"Yeah," said Martin. "But we need to be quick, because I think I can hear them outside."

Martin was right, there was a strange noise on the other side of the door, like people **moaning and groaning** (ächzend und stöhnend) and that noise was getting closer.

Henry looked around the room again. These were his employees. This was his team. He needed to help them now. He needed to be their team leader. "Right," he said. "Here's what we need to do. Martin and Derek, I want you to move the **filing cabinet** (Aktenschrank) and put it in front of the door." The two employees ran to the cabinet and started to move it.

"But how will we get out?" asked Mary, who looked quite scared. "The window?"

Henry shook his head. "Too dangerous. We need to go through the **AC system** (Klimaanlage (‚AC' ist die Abkürzung für ‚air conditioning')),” he said, and he looked up at the **vent** (Öffnung) in the ceiling. "Tim, Sally; move the table under the vent. We're going to **escape** (flüchten) from here into the reception area. From there, we can get to the emergency stairs. If we can go down the stairs, we can get to the car park and into the **company van** (Firmentransporter)."

"But," said Chris, the head of IT. "The video said they were outside, too. Maybe we should just stay here? We're safe in here."

Henry moved to Chris and put his hand on his shoulder. "It might be safe now, but soon they'll come through that door. This is the best plan."

"The vent's ready, boss," said Tim. "Do you want me to go first?"

"No. I'll go," he said, and he **climbed onto** (kletterte auf) the table and looked around the room. The strange noises in the **corridor** (Flur) were closer now, and he could hear something **banging** (schlagen) and pushing on the door. "This is it, guys. I need you to **trust** (vertrauen) me. Tim, wait until everyone is in, then close the vent behind you."

Everyone nodded. They looked scared but motivated, and Henry was **proud of** (stolz auf) every one of them. He **reached up** (streckte sich nach oben) to the vent and pulled himself in. It was dark inside, but there was enough space for him to start **crawling** (krabbeln) in the direction of the reception area.

For a few minutes, they crawled in the **darkness** (Dunkelheit), then, in front of them, Henry saw light from another vent. He turned back to his team and held up a hand. "I'm going to climb down and see if it's safe." He opened the vent and **lowered himself down** (sich nach unten lassen). There was no table under him this time, so he had to jump, and when he **landed** (landete), he looked around to make sure he hadn't been heard. For a moment, he thought he was OK, but then he heard that strange groaning and moaning sound coming from the entrance to the reception. He **froze** ((hier:) erstarrte), suddenly scared, but when he saw the **shadow** (Schatten) of something moving towards the entrance, he ran and closed the door. He looked around the reception area, then pushed the sofa in front of the door. Finally, he pushed a filing cabinet under the vent and called up to the guys, "You can come down."

When they were all down, he told them his plan. "I want Tim, Martin and Sally to go to the windows on the north side of the building and start making as much noise as you can. Mary, I need you to go behind reception and get the keys to the company van. Everyone else needs to move to the emergency

Hoffentlich
stairs. **Hopefully** the noise will make those things move to the north of the building while we escape to the south."

After a second, the guys started to bang on the windows and Mary found the keys, the rest of the team moved quietly down the stairs.

Es funktioniert
"**It's working**, boss," said Tim. "But there's lots of them, we need to be quick."

"OK, let's do this," he said, and then they were running down the stairs and Henry shouted for the rest of the team to go, and they pushed open the door to the car park and ran out into the sun.

"Go!" shouted Henry, who stopped at the door and held it open. Then they were all out and moving towards the van, but as they were going Henry saw some of those horrible things
um die Ecke kommen
coming around the corner of the building.

And that was when Mary fell. She was the last of the group running towards the van and the others didn't see her fall.

Still standing at the door, Henry knew he had to do something.

"Hey," he shouted, running towards her. "Over here!" Three ugly, terrifying heads turned to look at him. "Run, Mary!" he shouted, and as he got closer to the monsters, he saw her stand and run to the van.

She was going to be safe. His team was going to be safe! And he smiled then, **even though** (obwohl) the monsters were in between him and the van. Even though there was no way he could escape.

And that was when the three zombies **reached out towards him** (nach ihm griffen), and he closed his eyes, ready to be eaten.

But then, suddenly, people were **cheering and clapping** (jubeln und klatschen). When he opened his eyes, he saw the zombies **take off their masks** (ihre Masken abnehmen) and smile at him. "Well done, Mr Hale. You showed some excellent leadership skills."

Henry Hale smiled too. "Thanks guys. You know, I wasn't sure if this would work. But this is the best **team-building exercise** (teambildende Aufgabe) I've ever done."

to be responsible for ...
verantwortlich für ... sein

to head/lead a team of ...
ein Team von ... leiten

leading
führen, leiten

leadership skills
Führungsqualitäten

to be in charge of ...
verantwortlich für ... sein

aggressive
aggressiv

impatient
ungeduldig

dishonest
unehrlich

negative characteristics
negative Eigenschaften

disorganized
unorganisiert

manipulative
manipulativ

intolerant
intolerant

egotistical
selbstgefällig, egoistisch

indecisive
unentschlossen

arrogant
arrogant, überheblich

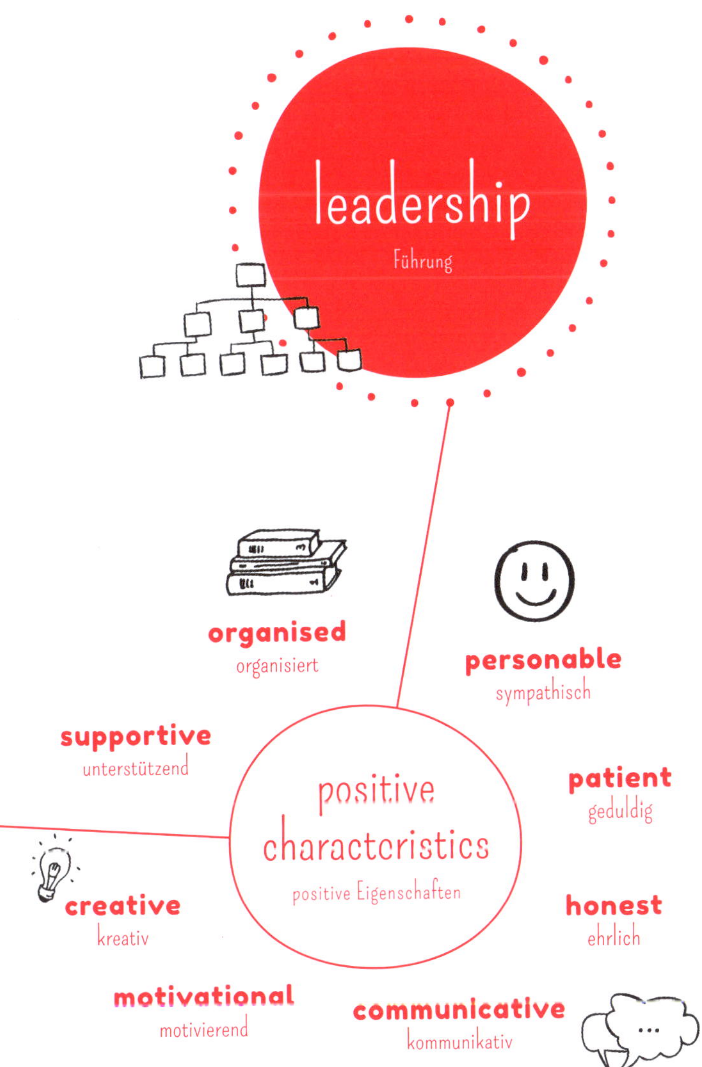
leadership
Führung
organised
organisiert
personable
sympathisch
supportive
unterstützend
positive characteristics
positive Eigenschaften
patient
geduldig
creative
kreativ
honest
ehrlich
motivational
motivierend
communicative
kommunikativ
...

The End of Mr Bennet

There was nothing very special about the day it happened. Dark clouds **hung over** (hingen über) the North East of England, stopping the weak sun from warming the country, and making the 33-year-old accountant a little bit worried. It was a Tuesday, but it was his **day off** (freier Tag), and he had got on a train at Whitby station so that he could go hiking on the Yorkshire Moors.

Now, as the train began to move, he looked at the clouds **unhappily** (unglücklich). If it rained, his walk would be **ruined** (ruiniert). The idea put him in a **bad mood** (schlechte Stimmung), and when Mr Bennet was in a bad mood, he was not a very nice person at all.

You see, Mr Bennet was a strange man. If you met him, you might at first think that he was polite but a little cold. He was very formal and he didn't like to make small talk. However, if you spoke to him a little bit more, you would soon **realise** (bemerken) that actually, Mr Bennet was a **grumpy** (mürrisch) and **irritable** (gereizt) young man. Now, of course, everyone **gets wound up** (regt sich auf) sometimes. Everyone has what we might call "**pet peeves**" (Aufreger); those little things that **annoy** (auf die Nerven gehen) us for no reason. But for Mr Bennet it seemed like everything was a pet peeve. For example, that morning, he **had awoken** (war wach geworden) to the sound of his milkman **whistling** (pfeifen) in the street. It was a rather nice whistle, and a lot of people liked hearing this **cheerful** (glücklich) sound; but not Mr Bennet. No, to Mr Bennet, whistling was an **annoying** (nervend) habit that made him quite angry.

Also, on the **escalator** (Rolltreppe) at the station, one man was standing on the left. This, to Mr Bennet, was **unacceptable** (inakzeptabel). Everyone knew that you stood on the right and walked on the left. When Mr Bennet saw this man standing there, he felt like shouting at him. And that was all in one morning. Normally, at work, he found seven or eight things every day that made him **furious** (wütend). For example, there were some people who tried to call him by his first name. He hated this. His name was Mr Bennet and that was what he liked to be called.

So, that was Mr Bennet; a very **cross** (verärgert) young man **indeed** (in der Tat). In fact, the only time he really felt happy and **at peace** (zufrieden), was when he went hiking in the countryside, which was why right now he was starting to relax and …

"Hi," someone said to him. "Can I sit here?" a young woman with bright pink hair, a nose ring and a big smile was standing next to his table.

"Well …" he said. "Yes, of course." He wanted to say no, because everything about the woman made him think that she was going to be very annoying. But Mr Bennet was polite. The seat was available and he didn't need to talk to her if …

"My name's Kate," she said, dropping her bag onto the table and holding out her hand.

Mr Bennet **nodded** (nickte). "Mr Bennet."

The young woman laughed and sat down. "Well, Mr Bennet, where are you going? Hiking?" Mr Bennet nodded and took out his newspaper. If he didn't talk to her, she would shut up soon.

"Well, I just want to go sit in that nice pub in Goathland. Do you know the place? I just go there and do the **crossword** (Kreuzworträtsel) and have a nice beer sometimes."

Mr Bennet **slowly raised** (hob langsam) the newspaper until he couldn't see the young woman and she stopped speaking, but then there was a sudden loud **crunching** (knuspernd) sound and Mr Bennet looked over his paper to see the woman pushing crisps into her mouth. "Want one?" she said, when she saw him looking.

Mr Bennet raised the newspaper again. **Chewing** (Kauen). He hated the sound of chewing. People should not be **allowed** (erlaubt) to eat on public transport, it really was the ...

There was a new sound now. He looked over the newspaper again. This time, she was **humming** (summen). Humming, in Mr Bennet's opinion, was even more **irritating** (nervend) than whistling.

For a moment, he tried his very best not to say anything. She seemed like a nice young lady, in a way. She had a friendly smile, and she was very pretty. Maybe he should try to be more **patient** (geduldig). Maybe he should try to speak to ...

But suddenly he heard the worst noise of all, and he let the paper drop. The young lady had put her crisps down and was now noisily **biting her fingernails** (kaute ihre Fingernägel).

"No!" said Mr Bennet, his voice loud enough to scare most of the people on the train. "Eating on the train! Humming! Biting your fingernails! Talking to a **complete stranger** (völlig Fremder)! You really are the most annoying person I've ever met!"

And with that, Mr Bennet stood up and walked to the far end of the train to find another seat.

Twenty minutes later, when the train **pulled into** (einfuhr) Goathland, he got off the train as quickly as possible and found the start of his **hiking trail** (Wanderweg).

Ten minutes after that, with the black clouds above him, he was on the side of a hill all alone.

"She really was very annoying," he said to no one. But ... he couldn't stop thinking that maybe the poor young woman had done nothing wrong. After all, she had been friendly, cheerful and she'd even offered him a crisp. Was it him or was it her? **If only** (Wenn nur) he could be sure. If only there was some sort of **sign** (Zeichen).

And it was at that moment that it happened. There was a loud **crack of thunder** (Donnerschlag) over the hill, and suddenly, without warning, a **flash of lightning** (Blitz(-strahl)) hit the hillside, and when the smoke **cleared** (sich auflöste), Mr Bennet was gone.

Except, that's not quite true, a few minutes later the door of that nice pub in Goathland opened and a young woman with pink hair looked up from her crossword. "Mr Bennet?" she said, to the man standing in front of her.

"Er ... no ... actually," he said. "Mr Bennet's gone. Which is fine, because he was a very rude and horrible person. My name's Jim. It's nice to meet you."

For a moment, the young woman looked at him like he was mad, but then she smiled and said. "Nice to meet you too, Jim. Crisp?"

annoyances
Ärgernisse
characteristics
Eigenschaften
over-sensitive
überempfindlich
irritable
gereizt
grumpy
mürrisch
choleric
cholerisch
moody
launisch
quick-tempered
aufbrausend
bad-tempered
schlecht gelaunt

pet peeves
Autreger

being late
zu spät kommen

sniffing
schniefen

biting fingernails
Fingernägel kauen

walking slowly
langsam laufen

talking about people
lästern

eating noisily
schmatzen

screaming children
schreiende Kinder

chewing with open mouth
mit offenem Mund kauen

useful phrases
nützliche Ausdrücke

to complain about something
sich über etw. beschweren

to annoy sb.
jmdm. auf die Nerven gehen

to be irritated by sth.
über etw. verärgert sein

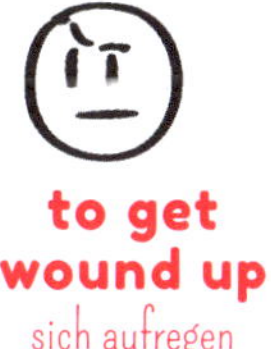

to get wound up
sich aufregen

to try to take sth. calmly
versuchen, etwas gelassen zu nehmen

to go up in the air
in die Luft gehen

A Grey Area

Grauzone

For a while, the university **corridor** (Flur) was dark and silent. Then, in the distance, there came the sound of **footsteps** (Schritte) and someone **quietly whistling** (leise pfeifen). It was Alfred Miller, the security guard for this part of the building. He had a **torch** (Taschenlampe) in his hand, and he shone the lights up and down the corridor before stopping to look at his watch. It was two o'clock in the morning and time for his tea break. With one final look around, he turned and walked back to the security room.

When his footsteps had gone, there was silence in the corridor again ... but not for long.

Suddenly, there was the sound of one of the large windows opening, and a figure dressed in black, with a **scarf** (Schal) around their face, climbed through the window and jumped down into the corridor. After another second, a second figure, also all in black, followed the first.

For a moment, these figures stood there, looking around **nervously** (nervös) and breathing quite loudly. Then, the second figure **pulled off** (zog aus) their scarf and a young woman took a deep breath.

"I can't breathe in that thing," she said.

The first figure pulled their mask off too and the young man agreed with the woman. "I know! How do **criminals** (Kriminelle) do this?"

The woman, who was in her late twenties, with curly blonde hair and nervous green eyes, shook her head. "Don't say that."

"What?" asked the young man, who was probably just a little younger and who looked a bit similar to the woman.

"Criminals. We're not criminals."

"Well, **Sis** (Schwesterherz). We are **breaking into** (brechen ... ein) Cambridge University. Most people would say that was a crime."

"This isn't about crime. It's a **question of ethics** (Frage der Moral)"

The man **sighed** (seufzte). "You say that about everything."

"Shut up, Sam," she said. Although she knew that he was probably right.

Her name was Claire Wilcock, and she had a bachelor's and

master's degree in Ethics. Also, for the last two years, she had been working as an assistant to the current professor of Ethics at Cambridge, Professor Edmund Kane.

"How can it be a crime if I'm taking back something of mine?"

"Well," said Sam. "The Einbruch **breaking and entering**."

Claire knew he was right again. "Come on then."

They walked quickly down the corridor and stopped at a large door at the end. "Do we abbrechen **break it down**?"

"No!" said Claire. "I told you, we're not criminals. I have a key."

Sam shook his head. "So, breaking it down is wrong, but using a key that you stole is OK? You have some strange Prinzipien **principles**, Sis."

"I didn't steal it. I ... I ..."

"Borrowed it?"

"Shut up," Claire said, as she opened the door and stepped into a small dark room.

They turned on their torches and looked around. It was a comfortable little Büro **study**, with a large desk, some old paintings and some other bits of furniture. "Urgh, horrible," said Sam. "He's got a Hirschkopf **stag's head** on the wall."

Claire looked up at the poor stag. "Yeah, well, that's why we're here. Professor Kane is a horrible person."

Sam laughed. "OK, tell me one more time what happened."

Claire sighed. "He's horrible. He gives good **grades** (Noten) to the students who are nice to him. He gives really good grades to pretty girls who are nice to him. I've heard him say sexist, **racist** (rassistisch) and **generally prejudiced** (allgemein vorurteilsbehaftet) things. He's horrible to any student from a poor family. He has no **moral compass** (moralische Richtschnur)."

Sam **nodded** (nickte). "So, you decided to break into his office?"

Claire started to look through the **papers** (Unterlagen) on the professor's desk. "I've been working as his assistant because I want to take over his job, yeah? Well, last week, when he was horrible to a student, I decided that I couldn't work for him anymore. So, I went home, and I drank a glass of wine ... or two."

"You mean two bottles," Sam laughed.

"Then I wrote a letter telling him exactly what I thought about him and I went out and posted it."

"So, what happened?"

"Nothing. I mean, not until this afternoon. He asked me to come in here. I was waiting for him to **fire** (feuern, kündigen) me, but instead he told me that he was **retiring** (in Rente gehen) in the summer, and that he was going to **recommend** (empfehlen) that I take his job."

Sam started to laugh. "It's quite funny really. Then?"

"I was thanking him for the **opportunity** (Möglichkeit) when I looked down and saw my letter on this desk. It wasn't open, so I knew he hadn't read it. And that's when I thought about this plan."

"Oh, Sis. You really are terrible."

"I agree," said a voice, and suddenly the lights came on.

Claire **blinked** (blinzelte), trying to see who had spoken. She could see the shape of a man next to the door. "Professor Kane?" she asked.

For a moment, there was no reply. Then, "Lucky for you, no."

And Alfred Miller, the security guard, stepped forward.

"Lucky?" asked Claire.

Alfred walked past Claire and looked at the desk. After a few seconds he picked up a letter. "Does this look **familiar** (bekannt)?"

Claire nodded her head.

"Well now, **on the one hand** (auf der einen Seite), you two have broken into a university to steal a professor's personal post."

Alfred held the letter up and paused.

"And **on the other hand**?" said Sam. (auf der anderen Seite)

Alfred nodded. "On the other hand, everything Miss Wilcock said about that horrible man is true. I've had to **tolerate** (tolerieren) his prejudices for years."

Claire suddenly had a feeling of hope in her heart. "So, you could say," she began. "That it was a bit of a grey area. You know, a question of ethics."

Alfred Miller nodded his head and looked at her for a moment, a small smile appearing on his face. "A grey area. Yes, it's definitely one of those." And he looked at them both. "And I'm just a simple security guard, so ... maybe I should let you decide what to do with this ... Professor Wilcock."

Then he passed her the letter, turned and left the study and there was silence in the university once again.

Well, apart from the sound of Claire and Sam jumping up and down and celebrating.

rights
Rechte

principles
Prinzipien

useful vocabulary
nützlicher Wortschatz

prejudice
Vorurteil

moral compass
moralische Richtschnur

tolerant
nachsichtig, tolerant

unethical
unmoralisch

abortion
Abtreibung

genetic cloning
genetisches Klonen

capital punishment
Todesstrafe

topics
Themen

animal testing
Tierversuche

social issues
soziale Themen

environmental protection
Umweltschutz

I see your point, but I think ...
Ich verstehe, was du/Sie sagen willst/wollen, aber ich denke ...

The main point I would like to discuss is ...
Der Hauptpunkt, den ich besprechen möchte, ist ...

talking about something
über etwas reden

On the one hand ..., and on the other hand ...
Auf der einen Seite ... und auf der anderen Seite ...

I'm afraid I disagree with your point.
Leider bin ich anderer Meinung.

Tell Me about Yourself

When the alarm went off at five o'clock in the morning, Peter Owen nearly forgot why he had **set** (gestellt) it so horribly early on that cold and frosty November morning. His hand reached out of the bed and began to hit the small clock until it finally stopped making the **sharp** ((hier:) schrill) ringing noise. When **silence** (Stille) returned to his bedroom, he smiled and **settled** (legte) his head back into his **pillow** (Kopfkissen). And, for a few moments, it looked like Peter Owen might fall asleep again. Then, suddenly, he sat up straight in his bed and his eyes **blinked** (blinzelte) open. "The interview!" he said, and a large and **enthusiastic** (begeistert) smile appeared on his face.

He pushed back the covers, pulled on his **dressing gown** (Bademantel), and jogged to the bathroom, turning on the lights as he went.

When he saw his face in the bathroom mirror, he shook his head. "That would have been a **disaster** (Katastrophe)" he said, thinking about how he had nearly fallen asleep again. “How long have I been waiting for this interview, now? Two months?” he laughed again, then began to get himself ready for what might be the most important day of his life.

Half an hour later, he was washed and dressed and sitting at his kitchen table. He was a tall young man with blond hair, lively blue eyes and a **clean-shaven** (glattrasiert) face. He was about twenty-six or twenty-seven, and if you saw him in the street, you would probably think that he seemed like a very positive and **ambitious** (ehrgeizig) young man; and **indeed** (tatsächlich) he was. You might also think that he was a successful business person, especially this morning, as he was wearing a blue shirt, a nice pair of black trousers, an elegant grey **silk** (Seiden-) tie, and a pair of leather shoes that were so **highly-polished** (hochglanzpoliert) you could see your face in them.

However, Peter was not a successful person. At least, not yet. In fact, since university, he had not been very lucky with jobs.

“But all that’s going to change today,” he said to himself when he finished his cereal. He poured himself a large cup of black coffee and looked out of the window. It was still **pitch black** (pechschwarz) out there.

He looked at his watch. It was now seven o'clock. The interview was at nine and it would only take him about twenty minutes to drive into Swansea. "But, **better be safe than sorry** (lieber auf Nummer sicher)," he said, thinking about the drive. "If I set off at eight, I'll easily be there by 08:30. Then I can find a nice café near the office, have another coffee, and think about my answers." He smiled at his plan. He liked to be **well-prepared** (gut vorbereitet) for things, it made him feel much calmer. "So, that means you have an hour to practise. And you remember what Grandad always says – **practise makes perfect** (Übung macht den Meister)."

He left his coffee on the table and walked into the small lounge. Opposite the sofa there was a large mirror on the wall. It was Peter's favourite place to practise. He smiled into the mirror, then he changed his expression to one that made him look **serious** (ernst) and **thoughtful** (aufmerksam). "So, Mr Owen," he said in a formal voice. "Tell me about yourself."

Peter smiled. "Well, what can I say? I **graduated** (machte meinen Abschluss in) in **economics** (Wirtschaft (im Englischen immer Pl.)) from Cardiff University and I have since been trying to find the perfect position to **suit my talents** (passend zu meinen Talenten) in this area.

I have a **passion** (Leidenschaft) for numbers, and I have three-years' experience working in **various** (verschiedene) roles. In my **previous** (vorherig) job I was **responsible for** (verantwortlich für) checking **accounts** (Geschäftsbücher, Buchhaltung) and making sure our data was correct. Also, I …" Peter began to say, but before he could continue a large **yawn** (Gähnen) came out of his mouth, "Oh, please excuse me," he said to his **reflection** (Spiegelbild) with a smile.

"And, would you say you're a team-player?" he said, in his serious voice again. "Oh, yes," he replied. "Absolutely. I think that I'm a great **communicator** (kommunikativer Mensch). I work well with other people, but I also know when to keep myself focused on work."

Peter nodded. That was good. That was the kind of thing people wanted to hear. He yawned again and **stretched** (streckte sich), then walked over to the window and opened the **curtains** (Vorhänge). It was still very dark outside. Dark and cold. He wished the interview was in the summer. He wasn't really a morning person, but a bit of sunshine might help him.

He looked at the clock again. He still had a lot of **time to kill** (Zeit totzuschlagen). Maybe, he thought, he should check he had everything he needed. Sure, he'd already checked three times the night before, but he didn't want to **leave anything to chance** (nichts dem Zufall überlassen). He walked back into the kitchen and picked up his smart, black bag. He had thought about buying a **briefcase** (Aktentasche), but he didn't really have anything to put in it. So, he opened the bag and did one final check. First, he picked up a brown folder and carefully opened it. There, inside, was a copy of his newly printed **curriculum vitae** (Lebenslauf), and he was very proud of it.

Next, he looked at the two **references** ((hier:) Arbeitszeugnisse) that he was taking with him. One was from his first boss, Mrs Smythe, the lovely lady who had worked in the newsagent's when he was a **paper boy** (Zeitungsjunge). He had wanted to get more references from the companies he had worked at since university, but strangely none of them had replied. Happy that everything was ready, he walked back into the lounge and yawned loudly. He was feeling pretty sleepy again now.

"Come on, Pete. You can do this," he said, and gave his **cheeks** (Wangen) a gentle **slap** (Klaps). "And can you tell me about your **strengths and weaknesses** (Stärken und Schwächen), Peter?" he said in the **fake** (nachgestellt) interviewer voice again.

"That's a great question. Well, I think my strengths are my

motivation and my **reliability** (Verlässlichkeit). If I say I'm going to do something, I ..."

Peter sat down on the sofa. He just needed to rest his legs for a moment. "Yes, if I say I'm going to ..." There was a **blanket** (Decke) on the back of the sofa. It was a bit cold in the lounge. It couldn't hurt just to keep warm while practising. He pulled the blanket over himself and kicked off his well-polished shoes. "So, yes, if I say I'm going to do something, I do it," he said, now feeling more **comfortable** (bequem).

"And weaknesses?" he asked himself, as his eyes slowly began to close.

On the kitchen table, steam was still rising from his large cup of black coffee. "Weaknesses?" he said to himself quietly, as he settled his head into the sofa. "None that I can think of."

job interview

Vorstellungsgespräch

at an interview

beim Vorstellungsgespräch

interviewee
Jobkandidat/in

interviewer
Interviewer/in

curriculum vitae
Lebenslauf

reference
Arbeitszeugnis

experience and qualifications

Erfahrung und Qualifikationen

I am/was responsible for ...
Ich bin/war verantwortlich für ...

I am/was in charge of ...
Ich bin/war verantwortlich für ...

to graduate
seinen Abschluss machen

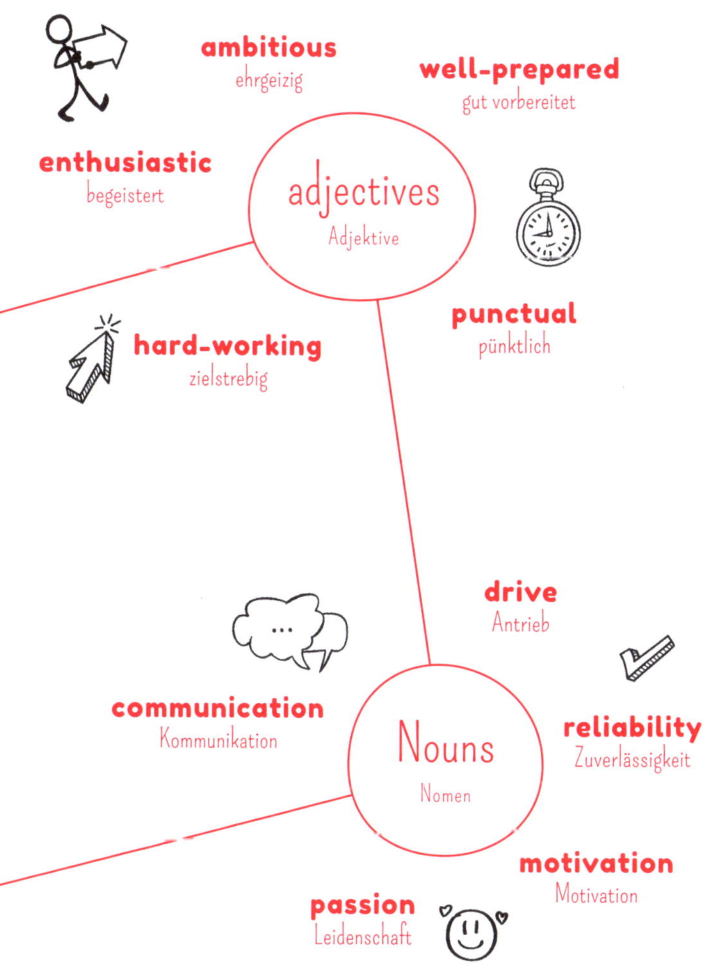
ambitious
ehrgeizig
well-prepared
gut vorbereitet
enthusiastic
begeistert
adjectives
Adjektive
hard-working
zielstrebig
punctual
pünktlich
drive
Antrieb
communication
Kommunikation
Nouns
Nomen
reliability
Zuverlässigkeit
motivation
Motivation
passion
Leidenschaft

10 Going Green

(umweltbewusst werden)

When her alarm clock **went off** ((hier:) klingelte), Debbie was up and out of her bed in seconds. With a **stretch** (Dehnen), she looked out of the window of her small cottage and smiled at the forest that she could see. The sun was slowly rising above the green trees and, at the moment, everything was quiet and still.

She walked downstairs to her kitchen and made herself a very healthy vegetarian breakfast of cereal and fruit, with a nice cup of camomile tea. When she had finished her breakfast, she cleaned her bowl and plate with some homemade soap, recycled the empty cereal box, and took the tea bag and fruit **scraps** (Abfälle) out to the **compost heap** (Komposthaufen) in the garden.

As you can probably tell, Debbie was very **environmentally friendly** (umweltfreundlich). However, you might be surprised to learn that this was quite a new thing. A year ago, she had never really thought about **global warming** [Erderwärmung] and **sustainability** [Nachhaltigkeit]. But then, one day, something changed.

So, she pulled on her boots, put a blue woolly hat over her curly blonde hair, and picked up her work bag. Then, without wasting another second, she left her cottage and walked into the forest.

It was early October, and already quite cool, but Debbie didn't care. She had a **mission** [Auftrag] and nothing was going to stop her.

After walking through the forest for about half an hour, she saw three familiar faces on the **track** [Weg] in front of her. She waved to her friends; Sally, John and Ian, and all three of them continued to follow the track. As they walked, they met other friends and familiar faces, too. In fact, by the time they reached the other side of the forest, there were nearly thirty people walking with them.

"Any **sign** [Zeichen] of them?" Debbie called up to a young man who was sitting on the high **branch** [Ast] of a tree.

"No, not yet," he said. "I thought they'd be here by ..." but then the young man stopped speaking and held a pair of **binoculars** [Fernglas (im Englischen immer Pl.)] up to his face. "Wait. Yes. Yes, they're coming!"

"OK, everyone," said Debbie. "Get into your positions."

The people around Debbie began to (an-)ketten **chain** themselves to the trees and after a few minutes there was a long line of Aktivisten **activists**. Then, Debbie took her bag off her shoulder and began to prepare something. When she had finished, she walked up and down the line giving each person a special homemade item and telling them not to worry.

But should they worry? Debbie asked herself. Yes, she had a plan, but she had no idea if it was funktionieren **going to work**.

It was then that two large Laster **trucks** and a black car stopped on the road in front of the forest. Debbie looked up the road to see if anyone else was coming, but the road was empty.

"Deborah?" she heard a familiar voice say. "Deborah Willis?"

Debbie walked over to a rather fat man who was stepping out of the black car. "Hello Arthur," she said.

"What's all this Debbie? Who are all these people?"

"Local people, like me, who love this forest. We're not going to let you fällen **chop down** a single tree."

Arthur laughed, but it was a horrible, unkind sound. "We?" he said. "You mean you're one of them now?" He looked around at the activists. "I hope you all know that Deborah was working for my company a few months ago. She helped us chop down trees all over the country."

"We know," shouted Sally. "But she changed, and so can you. You all can. You don't need to do this."

"You saw the plans for the new hotel," he said to Debbie, **angrily** (aufgeregt).

"Yes," said Debbie. "And when I saw them, I knew that everything your company does is **selfish** (selbstsüchtig) and horrible. You need to start thinking about the environment."

Arthur laughed again. "Stupid woman. You had a good career with us. What are you going to do with your life now? Spend it **hugging** (umarmen) trees?" He **clicked** (schnipste) his fingers and workmen started to climb out of the trucks.

Debbie walked back to her friends and looked at her watch. She was beginning to think that her plan wasn't going to work. Then, however, she saw another car **pull up** (ankommen) behind the trucks and a familiar woman and a man with a television camera got out.

It was time to be active, Debbie knew. She pulled a megaphone out of her bag and held it to her mouth. "My name is Deborah

Willis," she said, and she saw the young man with the camera point it in her direction. "I need to tell you that what you are about to do is not only bad for the environment, bad for the local people and bad for your **souls** (Seelen) ..."

A few of the men in the trucks laughed at this, and Arthur smiled. "It is also bad for you. You see, what Arthur wants you to do ... is illegal. He doesn't have the correct **planning permission** (Baugenehmigung) to cut down this forest. The documents he has are **fake** (gefälscht). If you cut down a single tree, you will be **prosecuted** (verfolgt) by the police."

"Don't listen to her," Arthur shouted.

"Is that true?" said the woman standing next to the cameraman. She walked over to Arthur and **held up** (hielt hin) a microphone. "Carol Haines, local news. Do you have anything to say?"

For a moment, Arthur **hesitated** (zögerte). Then, with an angry **growl** (Knurren), he turned away from the reporter and started to walk back to his car. But the workmen were still walking slowly towards the trees, many of them not sure what they should do.

"Now!" Debbie shouted, and suddenly the activists began to throw strange little bags.

The first bag missed one of the men, but the second one hit him on the **chest** (Brustkorb) and **exploded** (explodierte) in a **cloud of green powder** (Wolke grünen Pulvers). The man wasn't hurt, but he looked a little bit surprised and stepped back. Other bags hit other workers too and they all exploded in little green clouds that got into the men's beards and faces.

"Forget it, **lads** (Jungs)," the leader of the workmen said, when he saw Arthur getting into his car. And as the workmen started to walk away the activists **cheered** (jubelten).

Then, Arthur turned around and shouted back at Debbie.

"You won't stop me, Deborah. We'll be back. You can't wait here forever."

But Debbie didn't reply to this. **Instead** (Stattdessen), she picked up one of her homemade, environmentally friendly exploding teabags and she threw it.

And before Arthur could move, it hit him right on the nose and the green powder covered his angry face. "I don't know, Arthur," Debbie shouted, with a smile. "It looks like you're going green too."

useful vocabulary
nützliche Wörter

environmentally friendly
umweltfreundlich

harmful
schädlich

activist
Aktivist/in

endangered
gefährdet

contaminate
verseuchen

solutions
Lösungen

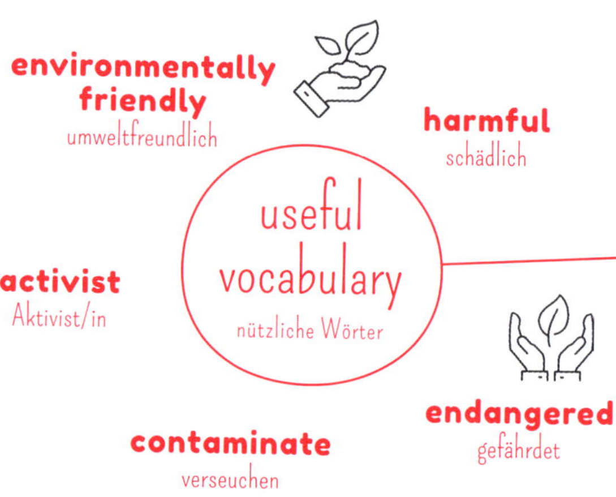

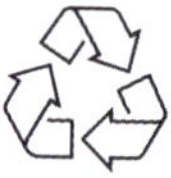

to recycle
recyclen, wiederverwerten

reducing emissions
Emissionen reduzieren

renewable energy
erneuerbare Energie

sustainability
Nachhaltigkeit

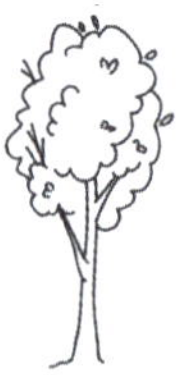

conservation
Naturschutz

reducing carbon footprints
CO_2-Fußabdruck reduzieren

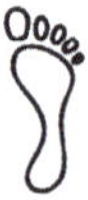

environment
Umwelt

issues
Probleme

pollution
Umweltverschmutzung

global warming
Erderwärmung

deforestation
Abholzung

fossil fuel
fossiler Brennstoff

acid rain
saurer Regen

nuclear waste
Atommüll

overpopulation
Überbevölkerung

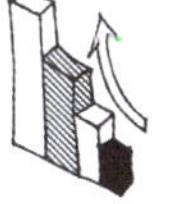

The Question

statistisch gesehen

"But **statistically speaking** ..." David started to say.

They were probably his favourite words, and Becky had heard him say them a thousand times over the last three years. This time, however, she wasn't going to listen; she couldn't. She turned away from him and left him standing in the rain at the **edge** (Kante) of the Scottish **loch** (See).

Quickly, she began the short walk back to the hotel where they were staying. **Tears** (Tränen) were falling down her face, but they were soon lost in the heavy Scottish rain.

"Oh, David," she said to herself, as she walked through the tall Scottish pine trees. "Why couldn't you just say yes?"

Because he never could, she thought, with a sad smile; and a memory of the first time they had met came to her.

It had been three years ago, at the **business conference** (Geschäftskonferenz) in Edinburgh. Becky was in the **audience** (Publikum) of a rather boring presentation about time-management. The speaker had been trying very hard to get the audience **involved** ((hier:) interessiert), and at one point she had asked someone if they thought time-management was important. "Well," a young man with big black glasses and messy brown hair had said. "Statistically speaking, most people are now better at managing time than they were twenty years ago. In fact, **surveys** (Umfragen) show that satisfaction with work-life balance has increased by 20 percent since 2000. The number of people working from home has **risen steadily** (konstant gestiegen) and ..."

The speaker on the **stage** (Bühne) had raised her hand. "I just want to know if you think time-management is important," she had said. The young man in the audience had **paused** (eine Pause gemacht) for a moment. "Well, **qualitative** (qualitative) reports show that ..."

The woman had shaken her head and moved away to ask someone else. Becky, however, had continued to watch the young man and, during the lunch break, she had gone to speak to him. "So," she had said. "You seem to be a big fan of statistics."

"I like the truth," he had said, with a nervous smile that Becky had fallen in love with. "If you have the truth, what else do you need?" Becky had smiled, too. "Some people would say you need love." David had looked a little verwirrt **confused** then, and she had never forgotten his answer. "But ... well ... what could be more truthful than love?"

A year later, they were living together in a nice little flat in Glasgow. Some of her friends thought that they made a komisches Paar **strange couple**, she knew. Becky was loud and lively. She had dutzende **dozens** of friends and could speak to anyone. David, hingegen **on the other hand**, was quiet and shy. He had a few nice friends, but he wasn't great at meeting new people. He got nervous. And when he got nervous, he began to talk about the facts and statistics that he loved so much. For example, the first time he had met Becky's parents, during a very nice dinner, he had begun to speak about chickens. "You see," he'd said. "The number of chicken farms has gone up dramatisch **dramatically** in the last 50 years. 60 billion chickens are now eaten every year around the world. Of course, the average chicken only lives for 43 days now and meat chickens are still klassifiziert **classified** as babies when they are killed."

Becky's mother had stopped eating, a fork full of chicken a few centimetres from her mouth. "That's ... lovely, David," she had said, before Becky had started to laugh.

Yes, sometimes it was funny and sometimes she loved his **passion** (Leidenschaft) for statistics. He worked for a large business company that paid him a lot of money for his facts and **figures** (Zahlen). She didn't even mind when he brought his work home with him, which he often did, leaving his **bar charts** (Balkendiagramme) and **line graphs** (Liniendiagramme) all over the kitchen table.

But this, she thought, well this was different.

"Becky?" she heard him shout.

She knew that he would be confused. He was a lovely man. Kind and caring, patient and honest. But sometimes he wasn't very good at understanding people. He spent too much time thinking about the numbers and the **percentages** (Prozentzahlen), but not about how people felt. She had said this to him once when he was preparing a report about a **failing** (erfolglos) family business. "Its profits have fallen," he had said. "They should sell the company now. If they do, they'll still make a small amount of money."

"But," Becky had said to him over a glass of wine. "It's a family business that's been **operating** (betrieben) for three generations. They love their customers. They don't want to sell it. They want you to tell them what they can do to help **improve** (verbessern) things."

David had said nothing for a moment. "But I've already told you. They should sell it. It's the right decision."

Becky had shaken her head. "No. It's the clever decision. That's not the same thing."

She reached the hotel and was about to open the door when she felt David's hand on her shoulder. "Becky, wait," he said.

She turned to him then. Like her, he was **soaking wet** (klatschnass). When they had left the hotel for their walk, there had only been a few clouds, and when the rain had begun to fall, they had run to hide under the trees by the beautiful loch. It had been so romantic, she thought; like something from an *Austen novel. In fact, the whole trip to the Highlands had been romantic. Maybe that was why she had turned to him and finally asked the question that she had wanted to ask for so long.

"You couldn't say yes, could you?" she said. "Why David?

Why couldn't you just for once say yes?"

David opened his mouth, but no words came out.

Suddenly, a horrible feeling filled her stomach. "You can't say it now, can you? You can't say it because you don't want to. You don't want to marry me."

And for a moment they stood there in the rain under the dark Scottish clouds and neither of them spoke.

Then, "I didn't say yes," said David. "Because ... statistically speaking ... it's normally the man who asks the woman," and David slowly began to **lower** (senken) himself onto one knee. "But more than that, I wanted to do it **properly** (richtig) ... with this."

And he took a small black box from his pocket, opened it and held it up to Becky, and he asked her the same question that she had asked him.

Then she gave him her answer and it was the truth; which David loved.

* Jane Austen (1775 – 1817) ist wohl eine der beliebtesten britischen Schriftstellerinnen aller Zeiten. Zu ihren berühmtesten Werken, die von den Irrungen und Wirrungen der Liebe handeln, zählen 'Pride and Prejudice', 'Emma' oder 'Mansfield Park'. Viele ihrer Romane wurden immer wieder verfilmt. Obwohl sie viel über Beziehungen und Ehen schrieb, blieb Jane Austen selbst in der Liebe glücklos und heiratete nie.

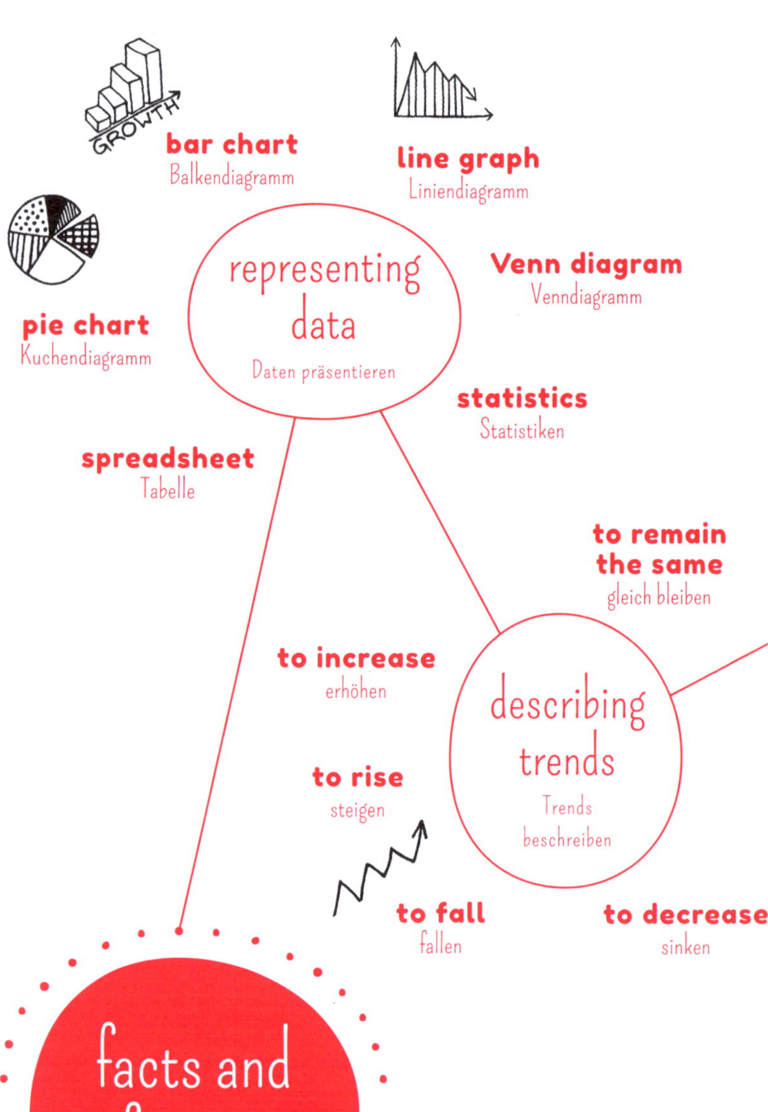

facts and figures

Fakten und Zahlen

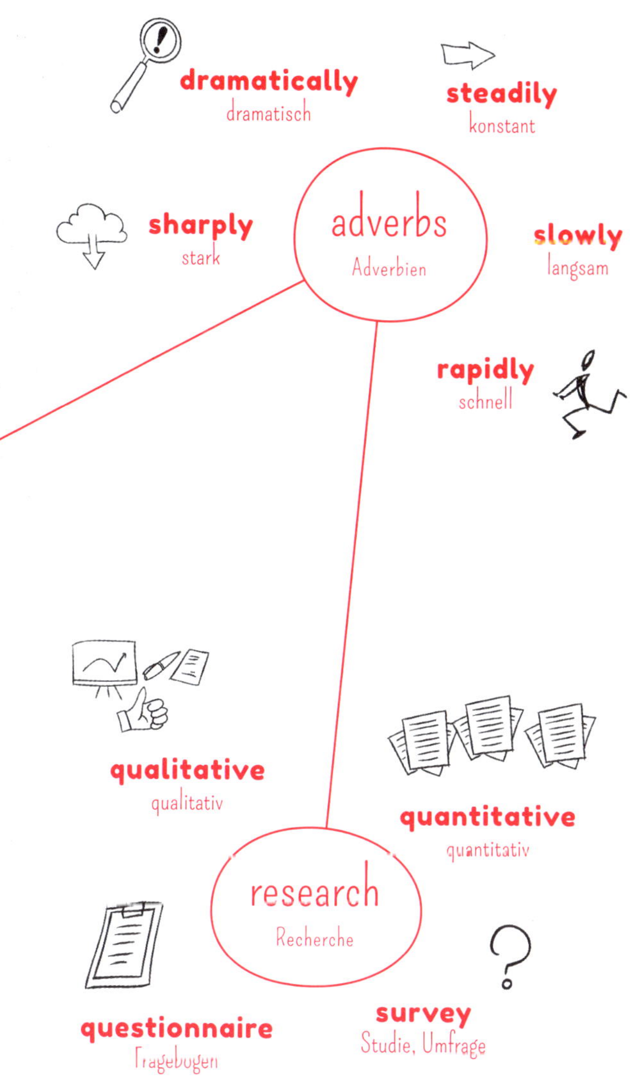
dramatically
dramatisch
steadily
konstant
sharply
stark
adverbs
Adverbien
slowly
langsam
rapidly
schnell
qualitative
qualitativ
quantitative
quantitativ
research
Recherche
questionnaire
Fragebogen
survey
Studie, Umfrage

Do it Yourself

Cathy watched her husband open the door and step out into the snow and shake his head. There were many reasons for her to still love Jim after being married to him for nearly twenty years. He was a kind, funny, **considerate** (rücksichtsvoll) man. He was a great father to their twins. He worked hard at his job, but always made enough time for the family. Also, he was a very **practical** (handwerklich begabt) man. Cathy knew that it was a bit **old-fashioned** (altmodisch), but she liked the fact that Jim knew how to fix and repair things.

Sometimes, **though** (aber), she felt that Jim needed to accept that he didn't know everything about everything. Yes, he could change a **lightbulb** (Glühbirne), **plaster** (verputzen) a hole in the wall and lay **tiles** (Fliesen) on the bathroom floor. But Jim had a **weakness** (Schwäche). He had an area of **DIY** (Do-it-yourself, Heimwerken) and maintenance that he was not very good at: technology. Sure, the simple things like changing a **fuse** (Sicherung) or getting the lights back on after a power cut, were not a problem for him. No, it was all of this modern technology that he had a problem with. He was terrible with computers and often lost his work because he never **backed it up** (machte ein Back-up). He found it impossible to record things on the TV in the lounge and always **ended up** (endete) **deleting** (löschen) what Cathy had saved.

Of course, none of this **mattered** (war wichtig) to Cathy, she quite liked new technology, so she would be happy to help him with it.

However (Jedoch), Jim was not very good at accepting help ... from anyone. "It's called DIY, Cathy. Do ... it ... yourself," he always said. "It's not called *do it yourself* until you have a problem, then ask your wife to fix it for you."

Cathy had laughed at this the first and second time he had said it; maybe even the third. After that though, she began to get a little bit **annoyed** (verärgert) with him.

And then, six months ago, the Robinsons had moved in across the street. They were a lovely family, Susan and Keith and their two young children Mark and Katie. Cathy had invited them **round** ((hier:) zu sich) for dinner, and she had thought that everything had gone

Zumindest
very well. **At least**, she had thought this until she had spoken to Jim later that night as they were getting ready for bed.

"Aren't they lovely?" she had said.

Jim hadn't replied.

"Susan's very nice. I think I'll see if she wants to join my Zumba class next week."

Again, Jim had said nothing.

"Did you like Keith? Do you think you two will be good friends?"

"Mmm," was the noise that Jim had made.

"Well? What's wrong with him? He seemed very nice, didn't he?"

Ich denke schon
"**I suppose so**," Jim had finally replied.

geseufzt
Cathy had **sighed**. "But?"

"But, well, did you hear what he was saying about our TV?"

Marke
"I heard him ask what **make** it was."

"Exactly. And then he told me what TV they had. Don't you think that's rude?"

"Rude? Jim, what are you talking about?"

Jim was getting into bed, but he looked very unhappy.

"**He was showing off** (Er prahlte.). He was saying that our TV was old-fashioned and that his was **state-of-the-art** (hochmodern)."

"I don't think he was, Jim. He was just **making polite conversation** (machte höfliche Konversation)," Cathy had said.

But Jim wasn't **convinced** (überzeugt), and two days later he came back from the shops with a **brand-new** (nagelneu) television. It had a huge **high definition screen** (HD-Bildschirm) and lots of **gadgets** (Zubehör).

"Need any help **setting it up** (beim Einstellen)?" Cathy had asked when she saw Jim sitting on the floor studying the complicated **instruction manual** (Bedienungsanleitung).

"It's called do it yourself, Cathy," he'd said, unhappily.

The next day, he invited Keith over for a coffee and **casually** (lässig) showed him the huge screen.

"Wow," said Keith, who seemed **genuinely impressed** (echt beindruckt).

"That's a nice bit of tech you've got there." There was a pause, and Jim smiled, finally happy. "It's just a **shame** (Schande) you don't have the right sound system for it."

"What?" said Jim, the smile **sliding** (entgleiten) from his face.

"Well, for something like this you need a **cutting-edge** (innovativ) sound system. You know, like the one we've got."

And that was the beginning of what Cathy called the tech wars. Over the next six months, Jim became **obsessed** (besessen) with making sure that their technology was better than Keith's. He threw out any **device** (Gerät) that he thought was too old. He spent a lot of their holiday money **updating** (aktualisieren) all the electrical equipment around the house. And, of course, every time Cathy offered to help, he would repeat his same old **phrase** (Ausdruck), "It's called do it yourself."

And now it was nearly Christmas, and across the road, the Robinson's house was **alight** (beleuchtet) with the brightest and most colourful Christmas decorations on the whole street.

"I really don't think that this is a good idea," said Cathy, as she watched Jim move a high **ladder** (Leiter) into position at the front of their house.

"Don't be silly," said Jim. "All I need to do is **hook up** (verbinden) these last **wires** (Drähte). Our house is going to be twice as colourful as the Robinsons' when I'm done."

"And do you need any help?" asked Cathy, one last time.

But Jim was already climbing up the ladder, a box of lights and wires held **awkwardly** (ungeschickt) under his arm.

Cathy walked back into the lounge and turned on their huge TV screen. She could hear Jim moving around on the roof of their house and she listened **expectantly** (erwartungsvoll).

When, after a few minutes, she heard him shout, then heard a loud **thud** (Rums), she was not very surprised.

"Er ... Cathy," she heard him call, and she stood up and walked to the front door. Jim was hanging **upside down** (verkehrt herum) from the roof, his foot caught in all of the wires that he had carried up there.

"Yes, Jim?" she said, with a **bored tone** (gelangweilter Ton) in her voice.

"I seem to have a small problem. My foot's **stuck** (eingeklemmt). Could you help me?"

Cathy said nothing for a moment, then: "Help you, Jim? But, darling, it's called *do it yourself*. It's not called *do it yourself until you have a problem, then ask your wife to fix it for you.*"

Then with a little smile she shut the front door and went back to the TV.

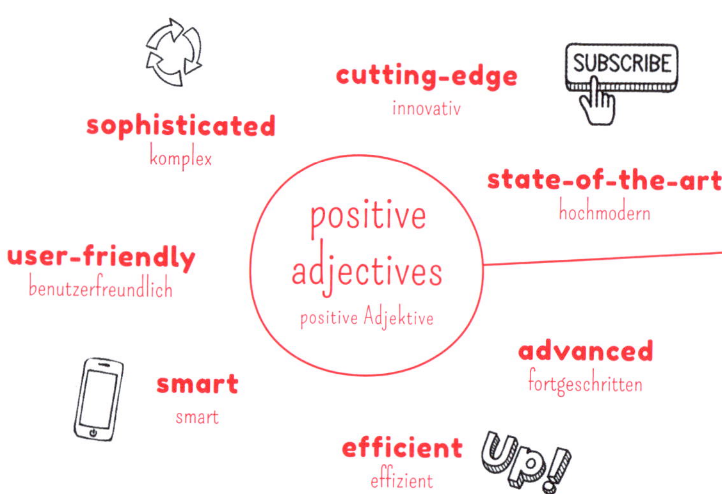

cutting-edge
innovativ
SUBSCRIBE
sophisticated
komplex
state-of-the-art
hochmodern
positive adjectives
positive Adjektive
user-friendly
benutzerfreundlich
advanced
fortgeschritten
smart
smart
efficient
effizient
Up!

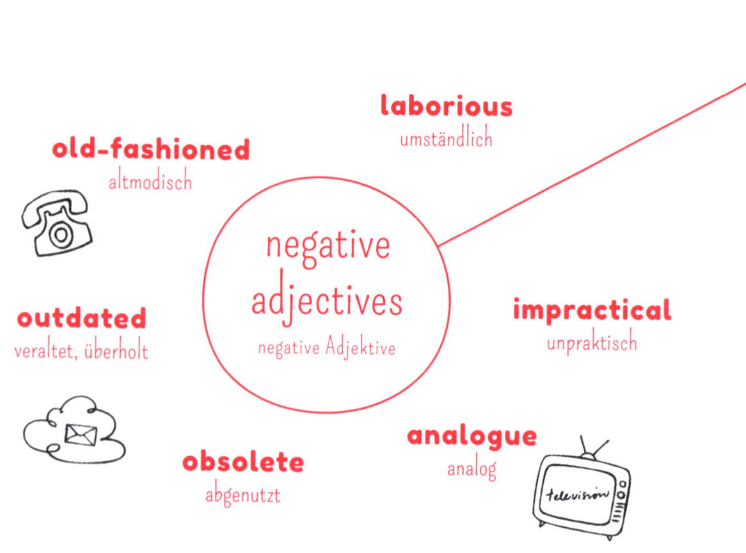

laborious
umständlich
old-fashioned
altmodisch
negative adjectives
negative Adjektive
outdated
veraltet, überholt
impractical
unpraktisch
analogue
analog
obsolete
abgenutzt
television

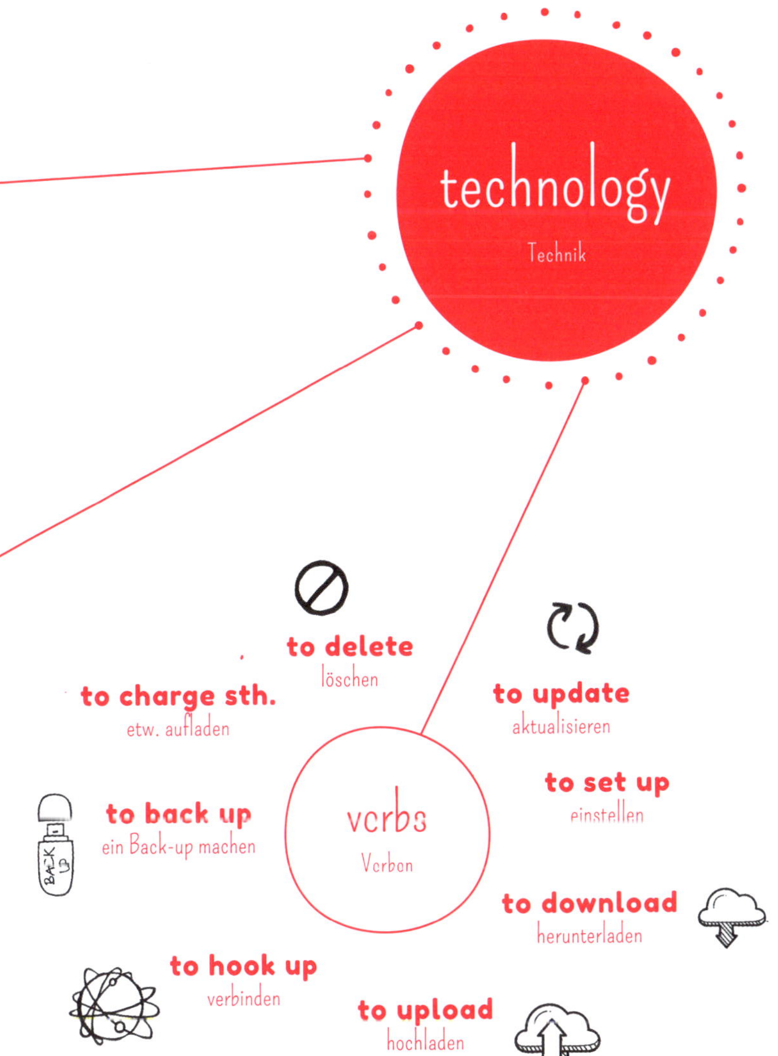
technology
Technik
vcrbs
Vcrben
to delete
löschen
to charge sth.
etw. aufladen
to update
aktualisieren
to set up
einstellen
to back up
ein Back-up machen
BACK UP
to download
herunterladen
to hook up
verbinden
to upload
hochladen

13

Just Another Day

Ein ganz gewöhnlicher Tag

It was a cold November evening in Sheffield, and PC Harris was about **halfway through** (halb durch) her final **patrol** (Streife) of the day. She had been **assigned** (zugeteilt) a quiet spot on the edge of the city; a boring but safe area where nothing ever happened. For two hours she had been walking up and down empty roads, **occasionally** (gelegentlich) **shining her torch** (mit ihrer Taschenlampe (be)leuchten) at some of the old factories that were in that area. She had been listening to her police radio too, but things were quiet that night. The only interesting report she had heard was of a **robbery** (Raub) on the other side of the city. The **offender** (Straftäter) had escaped and there had been a warning that all officers should **keep an eye out** (Ausschau halten) for the **suspect** (Verdächtiger). Harris doubted that he would **end up** ((hier:) auftauchen) anywhere near here, but maybe it was because of the warning that she felt a little bit **jumpier** (schreckhaft) than usual.

"It's just another day," she said to herself as she lifted her torch to see what was moving behind a tall, **rusty** (rostig) fence. It was just a cat, and Harris smiled.

She was a young woman of no more than thirty. She was slim, with dark hair and dark eyes, and in her police uniform she looked very serious and very professional. Still, there were times when she felt like she had a lot to learn about the job.

She watched the cat move away and she was about to continue her patrol, when a loud scream filled the dark street.

She **spun around** (drehte sich um), the torch moving from left to right. The scream had **echoed** (gehallt) around the old factories and she wasn't sure where it had come from. For a second, there was silence, then another scream **ripped into** (schallte) the darkness.

She moved her hand to her radio, then stopped. She couldn't **report the crime** (das Verbrechen melden) if she didn't know what was happening.

Was somebody hurt? Did they need an ambulance?

Or, she thought, suddenly a little nervous again, was it the **robber** (Räuber)? Was he **committing another crime** (wieder ein Verbrechen begehen) right now?

Quickly, she began to walk down the street, now sure that the screams were coming from that direction. There were no street-lights here, so she could only see where she was going by the light from her torch and from the **pale** (blass) moon.

When another scream filled the silence, she turned to her left. There was a dark **alley** (Gasse), and it sounded like the screams were coming from the other end. **Cautiously** (Vorsichtig), she began to move forwards, her torch held high, her eyes quickly moving from left to right.

And that was when it happened. A short man in dark clothes appeared at the end of the alley. For a second, he looked confused. Then, without saying a word he began to run in her direction. Harris felt her **heart leap** (Herz höher schlagen). This was the kind of situation that all officers **dreaded** (fürchteten). "Stop," she said, her voice **firm** (bestimmt) but not loud enough. "Stop!" she repeated.

But the man was still moving in her direction, and with the torch in her left hand she let her right hand move down towards the **taser** (Elektroschocker) at her belt. "Stop!" she shouted one last time.

And this time, the man did.

He was only a couple of metres from her and his eyes moved to her hand at her belt. "That's right," Harris said. "Stay where you are, please. I don't want to use this, but I will if I have to."

The man was Asian, with dark hair and dark eyes. He was dressed casually in dark jeans and a dark T-shirt. He had a wild and **panicked expression** (panischer Gesichtsausdruck).

"Can you tell me your name, please?" Harris asked. The man said nothing, but he turned around to look back down the alley.

"Sir? Do you need **police assistance** (polizeiliche Hilfe)? Has there been a crime? I heard somebody screaming. Has there been an accident? Do I need to **call an ambulance** (einen Rettungswagen rufen)?"

Again the man said nothing, but this time he raised his hands and he pointed back down the alley. Harris was about to ask him what he was looking at, when suddenly she **gasped** (nach Luft schnappte) and stepped backwards.

She had seen something that had made her skin go cold. "Sir," she said, her hand closer to her taser now. "What's on your hands?" and she **shone** (schien) the light of her torch onto his fingers. They were covered in something red, and Harris thought she knew what it was. "Whose blood is that?"

The man looked scared now, but still he said nothing.

"Don't move. I'm going to report this to the station and see ..."

But before Harris could finish speaking, the man turned and ran.

"Stop!" shouted Harris.

Then, she was running after him into the dark, the light from her torch jumping from side to side, her heart beating faster and faster with every step. She should stop and call for Verstärkung **backup** she knew, but she didn't want to lose the man in the many Seitenstraßen **backstreets** and empty factories.

"Stop!" she shouted once, when she saw him turn right down another alley.

But the man didn't turn around and when she reached the alley and shone her light down it, he was gone.

For a moment, Harris stood there, looking from right to left, trying to zu Atem kommen **catch her breath** and think. Then the man's head suddenly appeared at a hole in the fence at the right of the alley, and he looked at her with that panicked expression.

Harris understood something then. He wasn't running away from her. He wanted her to follow him.

Still nervous, she moved forwards and **stepped through** (machte einen Schritt durch) the hole in the fence. There was an empty road on the other side of it. Empty, **apart from** (außer) a small car that was parked to one side of it. There was a light on in the car and Harris followed the man over to it.

With his bloody hands, the man opened the back door of the car, and Harris slowly moved forwards and shone her light into it.

"Thank God," the woman in the back of the car said. "The car **broke down** (hatte eine Panne). We didn't know where we were." She was a young Asian woman with a very pale and tired face. She was half sitting and half lying in the back of the car, and there was blood on her dress and on the **blanket** (Decke) that she was holding in her arms.

"Kenji was amazing, but I was worried that he wouldn't be able to find help. He doesn't speak a word of English. Thank you for coming," said the young tourist.

And as Harris moved her torch down to the blankets that the woman was holding so carefully, the **newborn** (neugeboren) baby began to cry.

"Oh, **it's nothing** (keine Ursache; nicht der Rede wert)," said Harris, "Just another day."

murder
Mord
shoplifting
Ladendiebstahl
vandalism
Vandalismus
crime
Verbrechen
fraud
Betrug
violence
Gewalt
burglary
Einbruch
robbery
Raub
arson
Brandstiftung
police emergency
polizeilicher Notfall
SPECIAL
POLICE

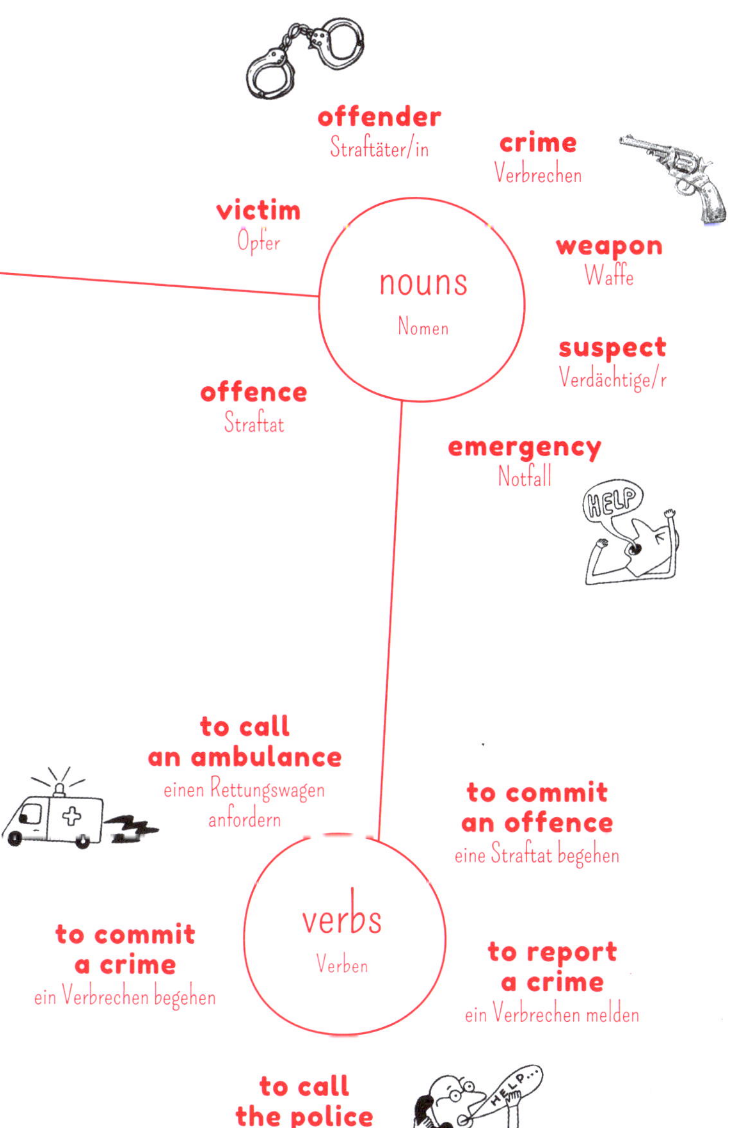
nouns
Nomen
offender
Straftäter/in
crime
Verbrechen
victim
Opfer
weapon
Waffe
suspect
Verdächtige/r
offence
Straftat
emergency
Notfall
HELP
verbs
Verben
to call an ambulance
einen Rettungswagen anfordern
to commit an offence
eine Straftat begehen
to commit a crime
ein Verbrechen begehen
to report a crime
ein Verbrechen melden
to call the police
die Polizei rufen
HELP...

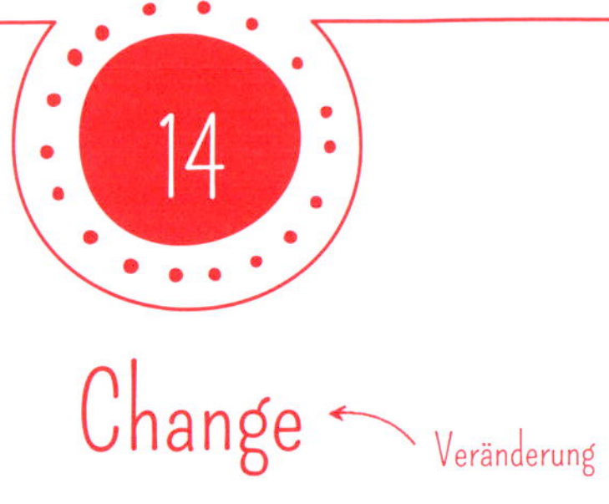

Change (Veränderung)

The small London **suburb** (Vorort) of Crouch End was busy that Monday morning. The sun was high in the clear blue sky and the **hands** ((hier:) Zeiger) on the **iconic** (kultig) clock tower said that it was nearly twenty past eleven. All along the street, busy but happy, people were **popping in and out** (gingen rein und raus) of the shops, relaxing with cups of coffee in the many cafés or stopping to chat to each other on the pavement.

At least (Zumindest), that was what most people were doing. **However** (Jedoch), there was one young man who was doing none of these things. **Instead** (Stattdessen), he was standing at the entrance to an **alleyway** (Gasse), not far away from one of the local banks. He wasn't moving from shop to shop and he wasn't saying hello to any of the people who passed him. In fact, he didn't move at all and he didn't **alter** (verändern) the dark and serious **expression** (Gesichtsausdruck) that was **half-hidden** (halb verdeckt) by his grey **hood** (Kapuze).

For more than ten minutes he stood there, but when he saw two police officers on the other side of the road, he moved back into the alleyway, pulled down his head and fluchte **cursed**.

"You can do this," he said, after a moment. His face looked younger now the hood was gone. His eyes were brown and worried, his hair light blonde and messy. He was thirty years old, or maybe a little younger, but the worried expression he wore made him look much older.

"You can," he said to himself, but there was Zweifel **doubt** in his voice. He took out a small black gun from his pocket and looked at it unhappily.

Then, the clock tower in the centre of town began to läuten **chime** half-past eleven, and the sound made the young man begin to zittern **shake**. He knew that it was now or never. He put the gun back into his pocket and moved to the entrance of the alleyway. Then, putting his hood back in position, he began to slowly walk towards the bank. His heart was beating faster and faster. Schweiß **Sweat** was moving down his face and falling into his eyes.

(hier:) Kleingeld "**Change**?" he heard someone in der Nähe **nearby** say.

The young man was closer to the bank now. He saw a woman with a young child enter and he felt his **stomach tighten** (Magen zusammenziehen).

"Change?" he heard someone say again. "Change? Sir? A little change?"

The young man stopped and looked down. A much older man with a grey beard and untidy clothes was sitting on the pavement. He had a small bowl in front of him, inside the bowl there were a few pennies and a couple of pounds.

The young man shook his head and looked back up at the bank. He put his hand into his pocket and felt the small black gun that was there. Then, "You don't want to do that," the **homeless** (obdachlos) man said, his voice quieter now.

"W ... w ... what?" the young man said.

The homeless man pushed himself up from the floor. "**How about** (Wie wäre es mit) a nice cup of tea instead?" he said.

And before the young man could speak, the older man put a hand on his back and gently moved him along the street to one of the small cafés. "Wait here," he heard the man say. And, not knowing what else to do, he watched the stranger go into the café and buy two teas. "Here you go," he said when he came out. "There's a nice park around the corner. It's only two minutes away. We can have a nice chat. Then, if you still want to do it, you can."

"Do ... do what?"

"Oh, I think you know." And he led him through the busy streets to a small park where things seemed much calmer and quieter.

"Darwin," the homeless man said, holding out his hand after they had sat down on a quiet park **bench** (Bank).

For a moment, the young man **hesitated** (zögerte), then, "Pete," he said, and they **shook hands** (gaben sich die Hand).

Darwin smiled. "So, Pete, what's this is all about?"

"How ... how did you know?" Pete asked.

Darwin **shrugged** (zuckte mit den Achseln). "You see things clearer when you live on the streets. I watched you standing in that alleyway for ten minutes. You were trying to hide your face from the camera near the bank. It wasn't hard for me to **guess** (erraten)."

Peter put his head into his hands. "I didn't want to do it," he said. "It's just that everything's become so hard."

"How?" asked Darwin, in a calm voice.

"I used to be a good person. I used to have a good job, a girlfriend, mates. But it's all gone now."

"What happened?"

"**Gambling** [Glücksspiel], mostly. I've always done it, but I started to do it more and more. I lost all the money I was saving for our flat, so I borrowed some from a **loan shark** [Kredithai]. They said I could pay it back slowly, but they **increased** [erhöhten] the amount so much that it was impossible. My girlfriend told me that if things didn't **improve** [verbesserten], she'd leave me. And I tried, I really did, but I just couldn't change."

Darwin nodded. "It can be hard to change who you are, to alter yourself. Hard ... but not impossible. I should know. I'm not the same man that I was ten years ago. I was something completely different, something I didn't like, but **I evolved** [ich entwickelte mich weiter]."

Pete looked at him, and he couldn't hide the doubt in his eyes. "And you're ... happy?"

Darwin smiled. "Very. I used to live in a large, empty house, all alone. Now, I'm always **surrounded** [umgeben] by people.

I used to have a job that I hated. Now, I do what I want. I help the council with local projects. I help other people at the Obdachlosen- **homeless** unterkunft **shelter**. I have time to think about life and what it means to me."

Pete looked at the older man. He really did look happy, he thought. "And how did you do it? How did you change?"

Darwin smiled again. "Like I said, I didn't change, I evolved. Entwicklung **Evolution** is slow and allmählich **gradual**. It's baby steps. You just make a small Änderung, Anpassung **adjustment**, then another small adjustment. Do you understand?"

Pete nickte **nodded** his head and stood up. "Baby steps."

Then, "So what was your old job?" Pete asked.

Darwin hesitated. "I'll tell you next time we meet ... perhaps."

Pete smiled a little too then. "Next time. OK."

And, as Darwin watched him walk away, he put his hand into one of his pockets and pulled out an old Namensschild **name badge**. He held it up and the words DARWIN JONES: BANK MANAGER, shone in the Sonnenlicht **sunlight**. "Still aufpassen **taking care** of the old place," he said to himself, with a laugh.

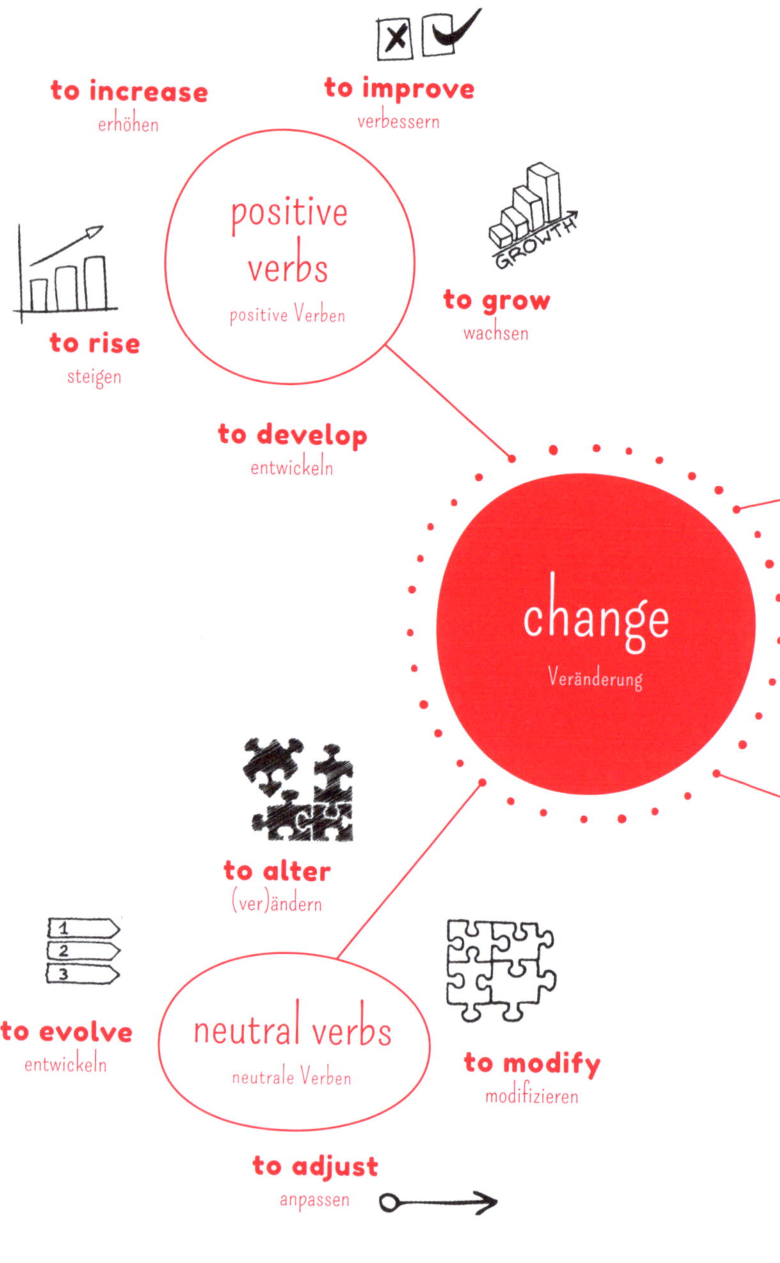
to increase
erhöhen
to improve
verbessern
positive verbs
positive Verben
GROWTH
to grow
wachsen
to rise
steigen
to develop
entwickeln
change
Veränderung
to alter
(ver)ändern
1
2
3
to evolve
entwickeln
neutral verbs
neutrale Verben
to modify
modifizieren
to adjust
anpassen

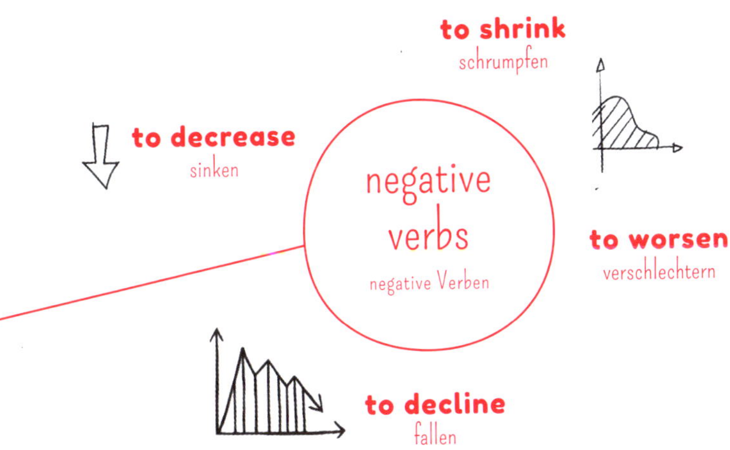
to shrink
schrumpfen
to decrease
sinken
negative verbs
negative Verben
to worsen
verschlechtern
to decline
fallen

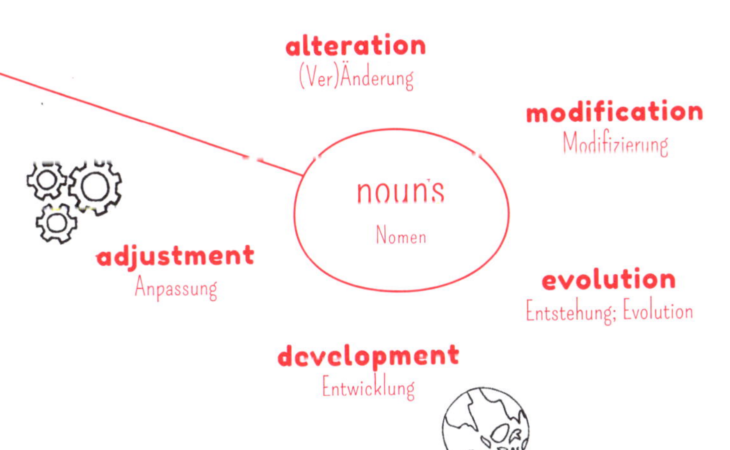
alteration
(Ver)Änderung
modification
Modifizierung
nouns
Nomen
adjustment
Anpassung
evolution
Entstehung; Evolution
development
Entwicklung

The Diplomat's Husband

"Say that again," Harry Wentworth said into his mobile phone. He was sitting in the back of a limousine, which was at that very moment **pulling up** (anhalten) in front of the Albert Hall in London.

"You heard me," said his wife, Caroline Wentworth, the UK's diplomat to Boranistan, one of the world's youngest countries. "You're going to have to do it for me, **darling** (Schatz). I'm so sorry, but I'm just terribly sick. I think it was something I ate."

"But you're never sick. Never. We've been married ten years and I can't remember you even having a cold," Harry said.

"Calm down, darling," Caroline said, kindly. "It's going to be fine. It's not even an **official event** (offizielle Veranstaltung). All you have to do is meet the Prince and his **entourage** (Gefolge) in the reception, make a little small talk, then watch the opera with him in the **private box** (Privatloge)."

Harry put his head in his hands. "Just make a little small talk ...

with the Prince?"

"Well, I do it every day, darling. Just be polite, taktvoll **tactful**, and ... well ... diplomatisch **diplomatic**. He likes to talk, so just smile, nicke **nod** and agree. Do it for England."

The limo driver opened Harry's door and stood waiting for him to get out. "But ..." Harry said more quietly. "I don't really like the Prince very much. He's ... well ... he's a bit respektlos **disrespectful**."

There was a pause. "Yes, well. Perhaps it's best not to mention that. Remember, smile, nod, agree. Now, I really must go. I'm not feeling ..." Then there was a Stöhnen **groan** on the other end of the Leitung **line**, and Harry heard his wife running for the bathroom.

Harry hung up the phone, stepped out of the car and richtete **straightened** his Smoking **tuxedo**. "Smile, nod, agree," he said to himself, looking up at the famous old building.

A few minutes later, an Platzanweiser **usher** was politely showing him to the VIP area of the Albert Hall's reception. "Look, everyone," he heard someone say, "it's the diplomat's husband. He's not as pretty as the diplomat, but he still likes to arrive late ... like a woman."

A small group of people laughed etwas **rather** too loudly and the

Prince of Boranistan **stepped into view** (trat ins Bild). "I joke, of course, Mr Wentworth." The Prince was a short man with a dark, tidy beard and an extremely elegant and expensive suit.

"I do apologise for being late," said Harry. "And, of course, I apologise that my wife cannot be here this evening. She sends her …"

The Prince waved his hand **dismissively** (verächtlich). "Yes, yes. But what can we do? This is why we don't give **positions of power** (Machtpositionen) to women. They are too weak and **fragile** (zerbrechlich). Am I right, Mr Wentworth?"

The small group of people looked at Harry, but for a moment Harry could not reply. He wanted to tell the Prince that his wife was the strongest and least fragile person that he had ever met. However, in the back of his head he could hear Caroline's advice. Harry smiled, nodded his head, and said something very quietly.

"What was that?" asked the Prince.

But, before Harry could say anything else, the bell for the start of the opera rang. "Ah, it's time to go to the box, your highness,"

Harry said, **deferentially** (achtungsvoll).

The Prince nodded and spoke to an usher. "Take us to our box," he said, and Harry **winced** (zuckte zusammen) at the **direct way** (direkte Art) the man spoke. A few moments later, Harry, the Prince and the small entourage were being seated in the best box. The Prince, however, did not seem very happy. "It's not very big, is it?" he said to the usher, who looked very nervous and didn't know what to say.

"And," said Harry, **catching the Prince's attention** (die Aufmerksamkeit des Prinz erregen). "Are you enjoying your visit to the UK?" he asked, **subtly** (unterschwellig) signalling that the usher could leave.

"It's cold and wet. Do you never have the sun in this country? Is that why you all look so pale and unhappy?" said the Prince.

Harry remembered Caroline's advice. "**I suppose so** (Ich denke schon)," he said with a smile and a nod."

A young waitress came into the box and started to pour the guests glasses of champagne.

The Prince looked at the young woman. "It really is a **shame** (Schande) that your wife could not be here. She is the best kind of diplomat."

Harry was quite surprised by this **unexpected** (unerwartet) comment.

"That's very kind of you to say."

The Prince smiled. "**In fact**," (Im Grunde genommen) he said, looking round at his entourage. "Maybe all women should be diplomats. Then, we would have something nice to look at, but nothing important to listen to. What woman has ever said anything important?"

Everyone in the box **except for** (außer) Harry and the young waitress laughed. Harry felt that he could not **bite his tongue** (sich auf die Zunge beißen) anymore. He was about to open his mouth when the lights in the Albert Hall slowly went out and the box was left in **semi-darkness** (Halbdunkel).

Then, "Champagne?" he heard the waitress quietly say.

"Of course," the Prince **snapped** (blaffte).

"Here you are," the waitress said. And there was suddenly a terrible noise of glasses being dropped and someone screaming in shock.

An usher ran into the room with a **torch** (Taschenlampe) and **shone** (schien) the light on the scene. The Prince was covered in champagne and champagne glasses, his face shocked and angry. "You idiot," said the Prince to the waitress. "You stupid idiot! Look what you've done!"

Harry stood up then. "Yes, this is **disgraceful**," he said. "**I'll deal with** her." And he took the waitress by the arm and led her out of the box and along the corridor. When they were far enough from the box he stopped and looked around.

skandalös

Ich kümmere mich

"What are you going to do?" asked the waitress, who looked quite worried.

"That **depends**," said Harry **thoughtfully**. "You see, some people might think you dropped that champagne **on purpose**, because of the horrible things that awful man said about women ... and my wife." Harry stopped for a moment and let the waitress think about that. "But, of course, we know that it was an accident, don't we?" he said, with a **wink**.

hängt davon ab

nachdenklich

absichtlich

Augenzwinkern

And then the waitress did something that would have made Caroline Wenthworth very **proud**: she smiled, nodded her head and agreed.

stolz

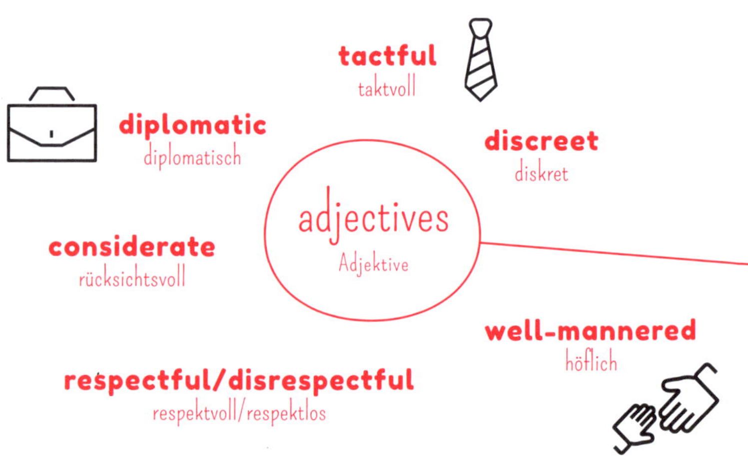
tactful
taktvoll
diplomatic
diplomatisch
discreet
diskret
adjectives
Adjektive
considerate
rücksichtsvoll
well-mannered
höflich
respectful/disrespectful
respektvoll/respektlos

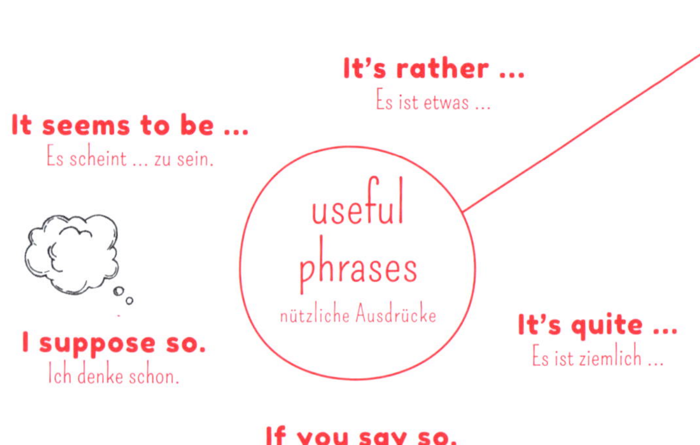
It's rather ...
Es ist etwas ...
It seems to be ...
Es scheint ... zu sein.
useful phrases
nützliche Ausdrücke
I suppose so.
Ich denke schon.
It's quite ...
Es ist ziemlich ...
If you say so.
Wenn du meinst/Sie meinen.

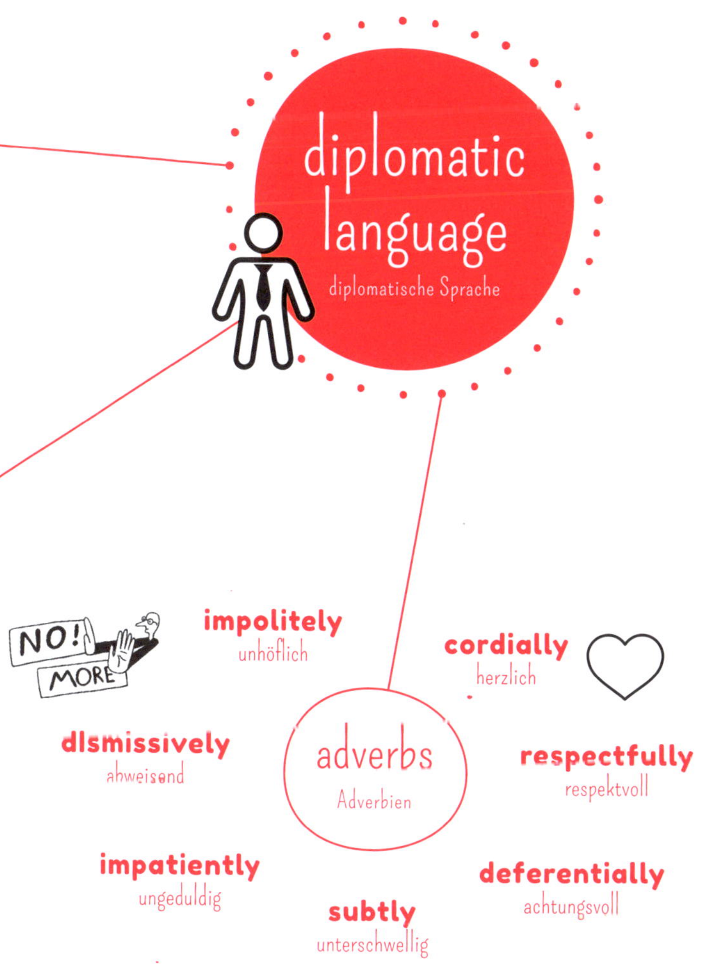
diplomatic language
diplomatische Sprache
NO!
MORE
impolitely
unhöflich
cordially
herzlich
adverbs
Adverbien
dismissively
abweisend
respectfully
respektvoll
impatiently
ungeduldig
deferentially
achtungsvoll
subtly
unterschwellig

BILDNACHWEIS

16, 24, 38, 62, 102 Shutterstock (mhatzapa), New York; **14.8,** 54.4, 63.4, 111.3, 111.4, 111.5, 127.1 Getty Images (topform84), München; **14.1,** 14.4, 15.2 Shutterstock (Natasha Pankina), New York; **15.5,** 22.1, 22.2, 23.1, 23.2, 23.4, 23.5, 30.5, 46.3, 54.6, 78.1, 78.2, 94.1, 94.2, 94.3, 94.4, 95.8, 103.1, 103.3, 118.3, 118.4, 118.5, 118.6, 118.7, 119.3, 119.4 Getty Images (Paket), München; **15.2,** 15.3 Shutterstock (Taxiro), New York; **15.4,** 102.3, 102.5, 102.6, 102.7, 103.2, 103.5 Shutterstock, New York; **22.2,** 23.3, 38.3, 39.3, 55.4, 79.4, 95.1, 95.2, 95.3, 95.4, 95.5, 95.6, 95.7, 102.1, 118.1, 118.2, 119.1, 119.2, 119.5 Getty Images (Dina Mariani), München; **30.1** Getty Images (Ollustrator), München; **30.3** Shutterstock (En min Shen), New York; **30.4,** 110.1 Shutterstock (Farah Sadikhova), New York; **30.2,** 31.1, 39.5, 54.1, 70.7, 78.1, 79.6 Shutterstock (topform), New York; **31.5** Shutterstock (Saint A), New York; **31.2,** 31.3, 31.4 Shutterstock (En min Shen), New York; **38.2** Shutterstock (Goodreason), New York; **38.1,** 39.1, 55.1, 55.3 Shutterstock (Valeriya_Dor), New York; **39.2,** 39.4, 70.2, 70.3, 71.1, 71.3, 79.3, 79.5, 95.1, 102.2, 102.4, 103.4, 103.6 Getty Images (fleaz), München; **46.2** Shutterstock (Natasha Pankina), New York; **46.1,** 47.2 Getty Images (macrovector), München; **47.5** Shutterstock (Aluna1), New York; **47.1,** 47.3 GooseFrol; **47.6** Shutterstock (Natasha Pankina), New York; **47.7** Shutterstock (Farah Sadikhova), New York; **47.8** Doodle Zeitung Buch: Shutterstock (Daniela Barreto), New York; **63.1** Shutterstock (artnLera), New York; **63.2,** 79.2 Getty Images (kostenkodesign), München; **70.4,** 70.6 Shutterstock (Netkoff), New York; **70.5,** 110.3, 111.1 Shutterstock (Macrovector), New York; **70.1** Shutterstock (alex74), New York; **71.2** Shutterstock (topform), New York; **79.1** Shutterstock (Toby Bridson), New York; **86.4** Shutterstock (primiaou), New York; **86.5** Shutterstock (primiaou), New York; **86.1,** 86.2, 86.3, 87.1 Shutterstock (davooda), New York; **87.2** Shutterstock (balabolka), New York; **87.3** Shutterstock (Multigon), New York; **87.4** Getty Images (veekicl), München; **110.2** Shutterstock (GooseFrol), New York; **111.2** Shutterstock (Canicula), New York; **122.1,** 122.2, 122.3, 123.2 Shutterstock (Set Line Vector Icon), New York; **126.4** Shutterstock (KateMacate), New York; **U1** Getty Images (RuthBlack), München; **14.2,** 14.5, 14.6, 14.7, 47.4, 54.2, 54.3, 54.4, 55.2, 62.1, 62.2, 62.3, 63.3, 63.5, 63.6, 63.7 Shutterstock (Maria Averburg), New York